IN SEARCH OF DAD

IN SEARCH OF DAD

CALLING FORTH
THE DAD WITHIN THE MAN

by

Charles Elliott Newbold, Jr.

Ingathering Press

Published by Ingathering Press
c/o Charles Elliott Newbold, Jr.
P.O. Box 31795
Knoxville, TN 37930

Unless otherwise noted, scripture quotations are taken from the King James Version of the Bible with certain words changed to their modern equivalent; for example, "thee" and "thou" have been changed to "you," and "saith" has been changed to "says."

Scripture quotations noted NAS are from the New American Standard Bible. Copyright © 1960, 1962, 1963, 1968, 1971, 1972, 1973, 1975, 1977 by The Lockman Foundation.

Scripture quotations noted NKJV are from The Holy Bible, New King James Version. Thomas Nelson Publishers. Copyright © 1983 by Thomas Nelson, Inc.

Scripture quotations noted NIV are from the New International Version of The New Testament, Zondervan Bible Publishers, copyright 1973 by New York Bible Society International, as found in The Zondervan Parallel New Testament in Greek and English.

The literal and more accurate translation for the Greek word *ekklesia* which is "called-out-ones" or "assembly" has been used rather than the traditional translation, "church."

The names of persons and certain details have been changed to protect the identities of people referred to in this book.

Library of Congress Catalog Card Number: 96-95019

ISBN 0-9647766-1-8

Dedication

To my faithful wife
who graciously makes room
for me to be
the husband and dad
God intended;
and to my children
who multiply the blessing
of family
by receiving
the gift of dad
unto themselves.

CONTENTS

Preface ix

Introduction: Looking for Dad 1

1 The Family Nature of God 4

2 A Family for God 10

3 A Family for Man 16

4 *The Dad* Power 27

5 The War against Family 33

6 Healing the Father Wound 43

7 Meeting Father-God 54

8 Becoming Sons First 64

9 The Dad's True Vocation 76

10 Elder Characteristics in the Making 83

11 A Man in Servanthood 94

12 A Man in Obedience 104

13 The Power of Affirmation 112

14 A Man of Blessings 124

15 A Man of Peace: A Man of War 136

16 A Man in Accountability 148

17 A Man in Surrender 158

18 A Man Who Does What Is Right 166

19 A Man Tested in Fire 173

PREFACE

When I read back through the manuscript of this book, I gasp! How could any man live up to the standards set forth here? My answer. Don't even try. Impossible! But with God all things are possible.

The idea of this book is that we can't, God can, so let us let Him—let us allow Him to do for us what He has set out to do anyway: call forth *the dad* within the man.

I have simply tried to paint what I believe is a God-given picture of what *the dad* looks like. All that any of us can do is look at this picture and say, "Wow! I want that"; then ask God to put us into that picture by putting that picture into us.

Faithfully and prayerfully read the ideas in this book and allow the Holy Spirit to convict you where you need to be convicted, change you where you need to be changed, encourage you when you need to be encouraged, and strengthen you when you need to be strengthened.

Small study group meetings

You can maximize the benefits from this study by using it in a classroom setting, a men's Bible study group, or an accountability group. Processing questions are provided at the end of each chapter.

Take time in your first session together to establish rules and guidelines for the meeting. The most important rule is confidentiality. Each group member must have the assurance that anything said will not be repeated outside of the meeting. Agree to be open and honest with one another. Accept one another unconditionally. Build each other up and affirm positive actions, decisions, and changes. Each person is to be responsible for his own thoughts, feelings, actions, decisions, and issues. No one person is expected to be a counselor but all are to be good listeners. Stay focused on the subject. Be regular and punctual in attendance. Set other behavioral and housekeeping policies that seem necessary and appropriate.

Allocate your time for the things you want to accomplish during each group meeting and stick to it. Meetings that go overtime discourage attendance.

During the week prior to each meeting, read a chapter of this book and, using a notebook, answer the questions for that chapter.

Suggested agenda for group meetings

Take an allotted amount of time to generally discuss the features that stood out the most in the chapter under study for the week. Share your answers to these questions: What ideas had the greatest impact upon you? What did you not understand? How did the contents of the chapter relate personally to your experiences?

Next, briefly share your answers to the questions for each chapter. Be open to other good questions that are raised.

Next, do any group exercises that are called for.

Finally, take prayer requests. Limit these to the issues being dealt with and being held up for accountability.

Pray for one another as you are led by the Holy Spirit and/or guided by the scriptures.

Pray privately for one another during the week.

Whether you are personally reading this book or studying it together with others, I appeal to you to stay open to what the Holy Spirit wants to do in your life. Invite Him to give you a spirit of wisdom and revelation knowledge each time you pick up this book to read.

LOOKING FOR DAD

At 58 years of age when I began writing this chapter, I was a father of three, grandfather of three, stepfather of three, and step-grandfather of two. And I was still looking for dad.

I did not have a dad for most of my childhood. He was off somewhere losing his business and being with other women. I have only a few memories of the time he was at home. I hang on to every one of them.

We were told that he was born the sixth child in a poor farming family of Elliotts in North Carolina. His mother died giving birth to the seventh child when He was about one year old. His dad could not take care of the children and had to break up the family. Daddy was taken away by the Albert Newbold family and raised in Pennsylvania. As far as I know, that is all he knew about his own blood kin.

Daddy grew up and had two daughters by his first wife. He left them and moved his trucking business to Kentucky where he met and married my mother. They had three children—my older sister, me, and my younger sister. I do not know why Daddy stayed gone from us all the time or why he and mother divorced. I guess he liked his women more than us since he soon became entangled in the web of another short-lived marriage.

He was my mother's only husband. He was bankrupt when they got back together and married again. Then, two years later, in the middle of the night, he died of a heart attack. I was fourteen. I was glad to have had him home

1

but in later years wondered why she had taken him back. She used to say that God allowed her to live out her days as a widow rather than a divorcée.

Raising the three of us was mother's solo mission in life. She did her best. But moms cannot be dads and dads cannot be moms. God did not make us both ways. So, I grew up knowing about mothers. I did not know about dads.

The grandpas had passed away before I came along. So, there I was: no dad, no grandpas, no uncles who cared, not even a brother. I needed a dad.

He had been dead for forty-five years, and I was still looking for him. I was looking for him somewhere down inside of me. I was looking for him in some tucked-away memory, some significant hug, in a good ol' behind-the-barn spanking, or in that moment of moments when my bigger-than-life dad would have called me out of my mother's hut, so to speak, to sit among the men of the tribe and have them say to me, "This day, young man, you have come of age." I would have grabbed hold of anything to add to those few faded black and white snapshots I had of him.

But that was then. In the months following my 59th birthday, God began to heal my father-wound. In the process, He revealed His own heart for family and how He is restoring the dad to the family in fulfillment of Malachi 4:5-6: "Behold, I will send you Elijah the prophet before the coming of the great and dreadful day of the Lord. And He will turn the heart of the fathers to the children and the heart of the children to their fathers, lest I come and strike the earth with a curse."

I lost my dad, first to divorce and, finally to death. My friend Jerry lost his dad to whiskey. Daphne lost her dad to twenty years without parole in the state pen. Ricky lost his dad to cancer. Clarisa lost her dad to the streets when drugs wiped out his job. Laura lost her dad to rage—one battering after another. Donny lost his dad to—well, he's not sure. His dad simply went away somewhere down inside of himself. Where have all the fathers gone?

Thriving societies are built upon the integrity of small family units. Thriving family units are greatly dependent upon the integrity of the fathers in those family units. The loss of fathering to one family is a loss to the whole family of man. The chain of society is as strong as its weakest link.

As we go searching for dad in this study, we are looking for more than a child support check or a dead-beat dad to slap in jail. We are looking for the father nature of God that has been sown into the soil of every male soul.

As we discover this seed of the father nature within, we expect God to put His desire for family into our hearts and restore family as He intended by first returning the heart of the fathers to the children.

This seed, this father nature that God gives will be referred to as *the dad* (in italics) throughout this book. The material in this book is intended to call forth *the dad* within the man.

I invite you now to join me in that search for *the dad.*

PROCESSING GUIDE

Write a brief paragraph describing the relationship you had with your dad and what effect, if any, you think that relationship had upon you. How has that relationship either prepared you or not prepared you to be a dad?

Write any thoughts and feelings you had while reading the introduction to this book.

Review the small study group meeting guidelines in the Preface before holding your first meeting.

Chapter 1

THE FAMILY NATURE OF GOD

The dad is embedded in the context of family as God intended family. If we are to unveil the mystery of *the dad,* we have to know family as God intended. Therefore, we begin with God.

God has promised to return the heart of the fathers to the children and the heart of the children to the fathers lest He come and strike the earth with a curse (Mal. 4:5-6). It is not in the heart of God to strike the earth with a curse. He intends, rather, to restore family as He intended family and to shower His blessings upon that.

Who is this God, and how can we claim to know His heart? I take the view that the Creator of the universe is one God who has made Himself known to key witnesses throughout the history of mankind. These witnesses bear consistent testimony to what God has said about Himself. These revelations have been recorded in the scriptures of the Old and New Testaments which serve as the authority for my claims.

I believe the statement in 2 Timothy 3:16 that "all scripture is given by inspiration of God, and is profitable for doctrine, for reproof, for correction, for instruction in righteousness." I believe that the concepts set forth in this book agree with the whole counsel of scriptures.

The integrity of family within God

Based on what Creator-God has said about Himself in revealed scriptures, I am confident to say that *God exists*

4

as a spirit entity with male and female identity and in-tegrity.

Not only is God both male and female, He is also father, mother, husband (bridegroom), and son. He is one God with these different aspects to His being. He relates to Himself within Himself in all of these ways. God has always been this way and always will be. This is more than imagery or metaphor. God is within His being, essentially, family.

These genders and family member aspects reside within God in integrity. By integrity, I mean they are of the highest standard for moral and ethical correctness; they are unimpaired, sound, whole, undivided, complete, and true. God represents within Himself what the ideal family looks like.

God as male and female

The evidence in scripture for the claim that God has a female aspect is thin, but I think sufficient. Our main clue that God is both male and female is first evidenced in Genesis 1:1 which reads "In the beginning God created..." The Hebrew term for God used here is *Elohim*. *Elohim* is the plural of *eloah* which is probably from the prime root *el* which means God or gods. It is interesting that this word is plural—God, indeed, has revealed many aspects to His being.

Genesis 1:27 reads, "So *Elohim* created man in his own image, in the image of *Elohim* created He him male and female." If *Elohim* created man in His own image—male and female—then *Elohim* is both male and female.

Since Adam was the first man created by God, he had no human father and mother—God was his parentage, both father and mother.

That God has a female and motherly aspect to His being is further disclosed in the title *El Shaddai* that He applied to Himself (e.g., Gen. 17:1). The Hebrew words *El Shaddai* have been translated "God Almighty." However,

5

some Bible commentators believe *Shaddai* comes from the Hebrew word *shad* which means breast and is always used in scripture in the feminine gender. *El Shaddai* speaks of God who nourishes and provides.

The feminine mother attribute of God is allegorized in Isaiah 66:13 where the Lord promised to vindicate Zion saying, "As one whom his mother comforts, so will I comfort you; and you shall be comforted in Jerusalem."

Speaking allegorically, Jesus cried out with the passion of a mother's heart: "O Jerusalem, Jerusalem, how often would I have gathered your children together, even as a hen gathers her chickens under her wings" (Matt. 23:37).

While God may be both male and female, we do not want to run amuck by calling Him our mother as some are inclined to do. According to the witness of revealed scripture, He chose to reveal Himself in the masculine and retained the position and function as the Father of His family.

Additionally, the male and female aspects of God are a spiritual reality which is far different from natural reality. We want to be careful not to try to understand spiritual matters with our natural, lustful minds. We need for the Holy Spirit to interpret spiritual things for us. Pray for that to happen.

God as father

The first Old Testament reference to God as Father is in Deuteronomy 32:6: "Do you thus requite [avenge] the Lord, O foolish people and unwise: Is He not your Father who has bought you? Has He not made you, and established you?"

King David knew God as Father. 1 Chronicles 29:10 tells us that "David blessed the Lord before all the congregation: and David said, 'Blessed are You, Lord God of Israel our Father, forever and ever.'"

Isaiah 64:8 reads, "But now, O the Lord, you are our Father; we are the clay, and you our potter; and we all are the work of your hand."

God was calling Israel to repentance in Jeremiah 3:19 when He said, "How shall I put you among the children, and give you a pleasant land, a goodly heritage of the hosts of nations? And I said, 'You shall call me, "my Father;" and shall not turn away from Me.'"

God declared his fatherhood very directly in Jeremiah 31:9: "I am a Father to Israel, and Ephraim is my first-born."

Psalms 68:5 declares that God is a Father to the fatherless. Psalms 103:13 tells us that the Lord is like a father who pities (has compassion on) his children.

The New Testament is replete with references by Jesus to God as Father—the same Father-God of the Old Testament.

The fatherhood of God is apparent in His discipline. Hebrews 12:5 reads, "My son, despise not the chastening [correction, discipline] of the Lord, nor faint when you are rebuked by Him: For whom the Lord loves He chastens, and scourges every son whom He receives."

God as husband

God spoke of Himself as a husband to Israel: "For your Maker is your husband; the Lord of hosts is His name..." (Is. 54:5).

The prophet Ezekiel captured in writing God's fury as a husband over his adulterous wife, Israel. "You trusted in your own beauty," God said, and "played the harlot because of your shame...Moreover, you took your sons and daughters whom you bore to Me and sacrificed them...You have slain My children...You are an adulterous wife who takes strangers instead of her husband" (Ezek. 16:15, 20, 21-32).

God finally divorced her after she repeatedly played the harlot and would not repent. He said, "And I saw, when for all the causes whereby backsliding Israel committed adultery I had put her away, and given her a bill of divorce;

yet her treacherous sister Judah feared not, but went and played the harlot also" (Jer. 3:8). In His mercy, God also declared, "'Turn, O backsliding children,' says the Lord; 'for I am married unto you: and I will take you one of a city, and two of a family, and I will bring you to Zion...'" (vs. 14).

God as bridegroom

In New Testament scripture, Jesus is clearly presented as the Bridegroom and His body of believers as His bride.

Jesus was talking about Himself as the Bridegroom in Mark 2:18-20: "And the disciples of John and of the Pharisees used to fast: and they came and said unto Him, 'Why do the disciples of John and of the Pharisees fast, but your disciples do not fast?' And Jesus said to them, 'Can the children of the bride chamber fast while the bridegroom is with them? As long as they have the bridegroom with them, they cannot fast. But the days will come, when the bridegroom shall be taken away from them, and then shall they fast in those days.'"

John the Baptist was talking about Jesus and His followers when he said, "He who has the bride is the bridegroom" (John 3:29).

The book of Revelation pictures the great end-time wedding that is to take place between Christ, the Bridegroom, and His body, the bride. "Let us be glad and rejoice, and give honor to him: for the marriage of the Lamb has come, and His wife has made herself ready" (Rev. 19:7).

Paul reveals this intended marital arrangement between Christ and His called-out-ones in 2 Corinthians 11:2 saying, "For I am jealous over you with godly jealousy: for I have espoused you to one husband, that I may present you as a chaste virgin to Christ."

God as child

How can we think of God as a child? Easy enough!

Isaiah prophesied, "For unto us a child is born, unto us

8

a son is given: and the government shall be upon His shoulder: and His name shall be called Wonderful, Counselor, The mighty God, The everlasting Father, The Prince of Peace" (Is. 9:6). In the fullness of time, the angel appeared to Mary and said, "You shall conceive in your womb, and bring forth a son, and shall call His name Jesus. He shall be great, and shall be called the Son of the Highest" (Luke 1:30-32).

God in Christ humbled Himself to the point that He was willing to be born into this world as an infant from a mother's womb. He grew up from infancy to adolescence, and on to adulthood. He was a child in the home of his earthly mother Mary and her husband Joseph.

Think about that! God Almighty subjected Himself as a little child to earthly parents whom He had created.

Jesus Christ came to redeem mankind for God. He finished God's work. He came as the Son to His Father because that is who He had always been to His Father. They are family.

Knowing God as family is essential to understanding what God's intentions are in creating mankind.

PROCESSING GUIDE

How did your relationship with your dad fashion your view of God?

How has your view of God changed as a result of reading this chapter?

How have the concepts within this chapter changed your ideas of how you are to relate to God?

How have you experienced God as male and female, father, husband, bridegroom, and child?

Write your thoughts and feelings about the ideas presented in this chapter.

Chapter 2

A FAMILY FOR GOD

God is essentially family within Himself. He made man a family entity like unto Himself. The families of men, thereby, mirror God's desire to have a spiritual family for Himself.

Mankind's natural families

"So God created man in His own image, in the image of God created He him; male and female created He them" (Gen. 1:27).

God said that it was not good for man (Adam) to live alone and that He would make him a helper. He took a rib from Adam and fashioned a woman. Adam saw her and said, "This is now bone of my bone, and flesh of my flesh; she shall be called woman [*ishshah* in Hebrew] because she was taken out of man [*ish* in Hebrew]" (Gen. 2:23). Adam, or *ish*, was both male and female before God took *ishshah* out of him. God separated these two aspects of *ish*.

The scriptures instruct that "a man shall leave his father and his mother, and shall cleave to his wife, and they shall be one flesh" (Gen. 2:24). *Ish*, having been created male and female, was separated, then joined together again in marriage. The male and female are compatible companions. Genesis 2:18 says that God made a help meet (mate) for Adam. The NKJV says that God made a helper "comparable" to Adam. The NAS uses the term, "suitable" which they say literally means "corresponding to." They naturally belong to each other.

10

The first thing God did after He created Adam (mankind) was to bless him and say, "Be fruitful and multiply, and replenish the earth, and subdue it: and have dominion over the fish of the sea, and over the fowl of the air, and over every living thing that moves upon the earth" (Gen. 1:28).

So, God made man, separated him to form woman, put them back together in marriage, blessed them, and told them to make family.

Set in families

God made us sexual beings—male and female—and placed us into families. He appointed that there should be male and female, husband and wife, father and mother, parents and children just as He is in His own nature.

The male-female couple is to reproduce more males and females. A man and a woman in our day grow up in different families, meet each other, are sexually and personally attracted to each other, find friendship and love, and decide to marry and have children of their own. In time, this couple dies and their children and their children's children carry on. That is the cycle of life. We are programmed as sexual beings to fulfill God's mandate to "be fruitful and multiply."

We find ourselves born into a larger network of extended natural family members consisting of grandparents, uncles, aunts, cousins, and so forth. We normally have a sense of safety in being a part of a family. Many individuals suffer loneliness and a loss of identity without family. We are social beings and find it impossible to survive socially, physically, economically, politically, sexually, emotionally, and spiritually without some significant connection to other human beings. Even when we feud among ourselves, we tend to stick together in the face of a greater threat from the outside.

11

God's desire for spiritual family

God revealed Himself throughout the history of man as our Father and wants us to think of ourselves as His children. In order to be His children, we must be born of His Holy Spirit. Jesus called that a second kind of birth (See John 3). We choose to be born of God by faith.

The first man, Adam, was created a living being but did not have the eternal life of the Father in him, though he had the potential for it. God did not want puppets, so He created man with the ability to make moral choices. He wanted sons with choice who would love and obey Him by choice.

Therefore, God planted two trees in the garden. One was the tree of life. The other was the tree of the knowledge of good and evil. The tree of life is widely accepted as being a picture of Christ. Adam would have chosen rightly had he eaten of the tree of life. He would have chosen the Father-centered life at which time he would have received the eternal life of his heavenly Father. He would have become more than a created living being. He would have become an eternal son of God.

However, because of the serpent's enticement through his wife, Eve (the female part of him), he ate of the tree of knowledge of good and evil. He chose wrongly. Rather than becoming a Father-centered creature, he became a self-centered creation. He lost his potential birthright in God and, consequently, was driven from the blessing that accompanied the birthright.

Adam's life and family fell under the curse. He had to till the ground in sweat, having lost his authority to take dominion. His son, Cain, killed his other son, Abel. The whole creation fell under a curse, and it groans to this day for the "manifestation [coming forth, revealing] of the sons of God" (Rom. 8:19-20).

Adam fell, but that did not change God's eternal plan and purpose to have a family for Himself. God's family, however, cannot consist of unredeemed, rebellious, fallen sons. They must be redeemed, obedient sons who are born again by His Spirit. So, He sent Himself in the form of a son, the only begotten Son of God, Jesus, the Christ, to show us the Father and make the way for us to be born of His Spirit.

Natural picture of the spiritual

Family is a picture in the natural realm of what God has intended for Himself in the spiritual realm. In His book, *His Ultimate Intention,* Devern Fromke expresses God's eternal plan to have sons for the Father, a body and a bride for His Son, and a temple (the body of Christ) for His Holy Spirit. Father, son, and bride are family terms.

Paul wrote to the Ephesians explaining that the godly marriage of male and female is a type of Christ and His bride. As such, husbands are to love their wives as Christ loved the church [assembly of called-out-ones]. Wives are to submit to their husbands as unto the Lord. Children are to obey their parents. And fathers are not to provoke their children to wrath; but are to bring them up in the nurture and admonition of the Lord. (See Eph. 5:22-6:4.)

Family is at the very heart of God's plan and purpose for all eternity.

The spiritual members of God's family

God is the Father of His family.

Jesus is "the" Son.

The general assembly of all true believers of all times is the mother. We often refer to her as "the mother church." I believe that she is the woman of Revelation 12:1-2: "And there appeared a great wonder in heaven; a woman clothed with the sun, and the moon under her feet, and upon her head a crown of twelve stars: and she being with child cried, travailing in birth, and pained to be delivered." Also, Paul wrote in his letter to the Galatians, "But the Jerusalem above is free; she is our mother." Who is "the Jerusalem above"? Rev. 21:2 says: "And I, John, saw the holy city, new Jerusalem, coming down from God out of heaven, prepared as a bride adorned for her husband."

The Son of God, Jesus, is the husband, the Bridegroom.

His true believers are His bride. The apostle Paul wrote to the believers at Corinth, "...For I have espoused you to one husband, that I may present you as a chaste virgin to Christ" (2 Cor. 11:2). He also wrote, "Do you not know that your bodies are the members of Christ?...He that is joined unto the Lord is one spirit" (1 Cor. 6:15,17).

We, as believers who have been born into the family of God, are also referred to as the children of God—brothers and sisters in Christ. Believers who are obedient to the Holy Spirit are the sons of God.

Indeed, we are the family of God. "Now therefore you are no more strangers and foreigners, but fellow citizens with the saints, and of the household of God" (Eph 2:19).

The wedding feast of the Lamb

The Bible begins with a wedding and ends with a wedding. As it was in the beginning so shall it be in the end.

First there was God, *Elohim*, who existed as a spirit entity with complete gender and family member integrity. *Elohim* is complete within His nature as male and female, father, mother, husband (bridegroom), and son.

Then, *Elohim* made Adam after his own likeness and image: male and female. He saw that it was not good for man (Adam) to live alone, so he took the female part of Adam out of his side and gave her back to him as his helpmate.

Likewise, God chose a family for Himself—Israel of old and the called-out-ones for assembly in Christ. He has expressed Himself in His spiritual family as male, female, father, mother, husband to wife, parent to child.

Just as He gave *ishshah* back to *ish*, so does He plan to give the bride of Christ to the Bridegroom, Christ, so that, in the end of the age, they two shall become one in spirit.

14

Jesus' prayer in John 17:21 will be answered: "...that they all may be one; as You, Father, are in Me, and I in You, that they also may be one in Us: that the world may believe that You have sent Me." The bride of Christ won't just be at His side; she will be put back into His side.

We will all be in God as the family of God in all the fullness and integrity of God. We will be one with Christ and God our Father, although we will be in our glorified bodies and will not have lost our personal identities. The family of redeemed man shall become the family of God so that what God intended from the beginning will be fulfilled in the end of the ages.

The final work of the Son, Jesus, is to deliver all things unto the Father. "And when all things shall be subdued unto Him [Jesus], then shall the Son also Himself be subject unto Him who put all things under Him, that God may be all in all" (1 Cor. 15:28).

PROCESSING GUIDE

Describe how the members of your family of origin modeled family as God intended.

Describe how the members of other families exemplified family as God intended.

How do you see yourself today relating to God as a member of His family?

Write your thoughts and feelings about the ideas presented in this chapter.

Chapter 3

A FAMILY FOR MAN

Ma Joad, in John Steinbeck's classic novel *The Grapes of Wrath*, tried to persuade her son Tom not to leave the family, "[Ma] said angrily, 'Tom! They's a whole lot I don' un'erstan', but goin' away ain't gonna ease us. It's gonna bear us down...They was the time when we was on the lan'. They was a boundary to us then. Ol' folks died off, and little fellas come, an' we was always one thing—we was the fambly—kinda whole and clear. An' now we ain't clear no more...Pa's lost his place. He ain't the head no more. We're crackin' up, Tom. There ain't no fambly now...'"[1]

Family is the boundary that helps to define who we are. We know who we are because we know where we came from. Knowing where we came from gives us a guidepost to where we are going. As Christians, we know that we are the sons of God because we came from God. We were born into His family by the Spirit of God. As sons, we have our destiny in Him.

Family when it is intact as God intended validates us and gives us our sense of identification and belonging. Love, acceptance, trust, faithfulness, safety, and peace are the kinds of things that define its boundaries and make family work—not such things as money, possessions, power, positions, and prestige.

The term "family," so far as humans are concerned, refers fundamentally to a man and woman and their off-

---

[1]John Steinbeck, *The Grapes of Wrath* (Toronto: Bantam Book, published by arrangement with The Viking Press, 1972), 434.

spring who live together in a larger society. They share goals and values, have long-term commitments to one another, and usually reside in the same dwelling. The term also refers to a group of persons sharing common ancestry.

The mystery of family

Despite my definition, the term "family" transcends description. It is more than a simple word category that describes a certain thought form in our minds. It is more than a concept or a term to define a social situation. It is more than a man, a woman, and some children living together and calling themselves family. It is more than a term that describes the social structure of a small unit of individuals living together.

Family is a mystery. A mystery is something that baffles or eludes the understanding. Marriage and family are like that. It is a spiritual, sacred union between individuals that bonds them as one in a dimension beyond words.

God initiated this mystery when He made man as male and female in His own image and likeness. He looked at the man and the woman along with everything else He had made, "And, behold, it was very good" (Gen. 1:26-31).

The writer of Proverbs, awed by this mystery, considered "the way of a man with a maid" too wonderful to understand (Prov. 30:18-19).

The apostle Paul wrote how the relationship between the husband and wife are like that of Jesus and His bride, the assembly of called-out-ones. Then, as though he himself were smitten by the awesome nature of this relationship and the impossibility of finding words to describe it, he concluded that "this is a great mystery" (Eph. 5:22-32).

The power of family

Family is a power when it is intact as God intended. It is an energy that comes out of who God is to make something work among us for good. When we pattern after family as God intends, we become the recipients of that force that makes it happen. We pattern; God empowers.

"Skip is out of control," the exasperated teacher said. "The other kids say he beats on his sister and that his mom is never home at night. He has no limits, no boundaries, and he pushes everyone else to their limits. His single parent mom refuses to discipline him at home or to back his teachers at school. Instead, she took a teacher to court on a charge of child abuse. The judge did not take long to make his decision. 'I understand this young man has been spanked over thirty times by different teachers this year,' the judge said. 'It took only one spanking from Mr. McClure for me to get the message. I don't believe the problem here is with the school system. I believe we need greater cooperation with the teachers from the parents. Case dismissed.'"

Where was Skip's dad? Don't know. Without Skip's dad in the home acting responsibly as a godly father and, moreover, without God in the home, the power of family to nurture, discipline, validate, and provide an identity were absent. Skip, consequently, was the victim of abuse—the abuse of abandonment. He was falling through the cracks.

The frustrated teacher philosophized, "The father is the primary one who teaches limits in the home. Kids who are generally the best ball players have dads at home to discipline them. Not all, but many of the kids without a dad have a bad attitude, are disrespectful, and push boundaries to the extreme. Limits are harder to teach without the male-limiting factor."

Healthy and nurturing family life builds character in individuals, and individuals build societies.

Family, as a power, is greater than the sum of its individual members. When God gets involved, "one can chase a thousand and two can put ten thousand to flight (Deut. 32:30). "A threefold cord is not quickly broken" (Ecc. 4:12).

When we live according to the plan and purpose of God, we will have the power of God available to us to work the plan, because He anoints what He appoints and empowers what He inspires. If we try to redefine family according to world standards, we will have to operate in our own strength to try to make that so-called family work. When God's power is not in operation, we have to rely upon manipulating and controlling others.

When we pattern according to God's plan, we have family the way God wants it to be, and we have God in our lives the way He wants to be. God makes the difference because He is the picture, the presence, and the power of family.

Terms and conditions of family

God determined the terms and conditions of marriage and family. He determined that a male and female were to be united in marriage. "Therefore, shall a man leave his father and mother, and shall cleave to his wife: and they shall be one flesh" (Gen. 2:24).

God determined monogamy in marriages. In the beginning, He gave one wife, Eve, to the one man, Adam. While polygamy was practiced among some of the patriarchs of Israel, monogamy had become the rule by the time of Jesus. Harper's Bible Dictionary states: "Hosea preached monogamy as a symbol of the faithful unions between God and His people. Malachi (2:14 ff.) took monogamy for granted....The ideal woman of Proverbs 31 moved in a monogamous society. By N.T. times Jewish husbands usually had one wife."[2] Proverbs 5:18-19 exhorts us to rejoice with the wife of our youth. "Let her be as the loving hind and pleasant roe; let her breasts satisfy you at all times; be ravished always with her love." The New Testament letters clearly advocate monogamy and reveal that such things as adultery, divorce, and fornication are the enemies of God, the Christian life, and family. (See Rom. 7:2-3; 1 Cor. 7:2,11; 1 Tim. 3:2; Titus 1:6.)

God determined that couples should remain married

---

[2]Madeleine S. Miller and J. Lane Miller, *Harper's Bible Dictionary* (New York: Harper and Brothers Publishers, 1956), 110.

for life. The Pharisees, seeking to trick Jesus, questioned Him about divorce. He answered, "Whom, therefore, God has joined together, let not man put asunder." They asked Him why Moses granted certificates of divorcements. Jesus answered, "Because of the hardness of your hearts ...but from the beginning it was not so" (Matt. 19:3-8).

God determined that children should be born to a husband and his wife in the monogamous marriage and that the children should be viewed as a blessing from the Lord. "Children's children are the crown of old men; and the glory of children are their fathers" (Prov. 17:6).

The context of family

The family is the proper context for providing its individual members with spiritual, physical, social, emotional, and sexual nurturing. God instituted the family to provide this nurturing. He never intended for the state to parent our children. It takes human beings living together as family to fill the coffers of children with validation and identification. Institutions that fail to provide family groups cannot do this.

The family is the proper context for child discipline as modeled in scripture. God is the perfect model for fathers who discipline their children, and the fathers are an example of how God disciplines us as sons. Deuteronomy 8:5 reads, "You shall also consider in your heart, that as a man disciplines his son, so the Lord your God disciplines you." Hebrews 12:5-7 charges, "And you have forgotten the exhortation which speaks unto you as unto children, 'My son, despise not the discipline of the Lord, nor faint when you are rebuked by Him: For whom the Lord loves He disciplines, and scourges [whips] every son whom He receives.' If you endure discipline, God deals with you as with sons; for what son is he whom the father does not discipline?"

I have heard parents say, "I can't spank my little boy. I love him too much." On the contrary, proper discipline is an act of love. The frustrated teacher who feared for Skip's future said, "Skip's mom, thinking she was defending him when she needed to back up the authorities in his life, probably assigned him to a life of crime and prison."

Proverbs 13:24 (NKJV) admonishes, "He who spares his rod hates his son: but he who loves him disciplines him promptly." "Promptly" can also be translated "early." Proverbs 19:18 charges, "Discipline your son while there is hope, and let not your soul spare for his crying." Godly discipline cannot be put on hold.

The family is the proper context for providing instruction and understanding. Proverbs 4:1-4 also admonishes, "Hear, children, the instruction of a father, and attend to know understanding. For I give you good doctrine, forsake not My law. For I was my father's son, tender and only beloved in the sight of my mother. He taught me also, and said unto me, 'Let your heart retain my words: keep my commandments, and live.'"

The family is the proper context for the children to learn about honor, trust, truthfulness, and obedience—instilling them with wisdom and values. Proverbs 8:32 reads, "Now, therefore, hear me, children, for blessed are they who keep my ways. Hear instruction, and be wise, and refuse it not."

The family is the proper context for the children to learn about God and the fear of the Lord. It is a hiding place for spiritual safety. Proverbs 14:26 asserts, "In the fear of the Lord is strong confidence: and his children shall have a place of refuge." And the often quoted verse from Proverbs 22:6 says: "Train up a child in the way he should go: and when he is old, he will not depart from it."

The family is the proper context where the members take appropriate responsibility for one another. Jesus fulfilled certain obligations to his natural family even while suffering the agony of the cross. He said to His beloved disciple, John, regarding His mother, Mary, "Behold, your mother!" From that moment on John took responsibility for Mary in his own house (John 19:27). Jesus must have been responsible for his mother as the first-born son, otherwise he would not have had the authority to assign responsibility to another.

The family is the proper context for passing down legacies. A child's traditions, culture, heritage, and inheritance come down through the family. "A good man leaves an inheritance to his children's children" (Prov. 13:22). "The just man walks in his integrity: his children are blessed after him" (Prov. 20:7). Each generation should be able to build upon the legacy left by the former ones. While most children want their dads to remain bigger than life, most dads want their children to exceed them.

Instituted in sacrifice

Family is a power from God. The first family of man was instituted in sacrifice. God personally performed the surgical ceremony that brought it into being. Adam had to give up something of himself in order to have a bride for himself.

God's promise of a son to Abraham was confirmed in sacrifice. Isaac was the son through whom God intended to fulfill His covenant with Abraham that he would be the father of many nations. Yet, God required Abraham to offer him up as a sacrifice and Abraham had to be willing to do it. In the final moment, God supplied the sacrificial ram. (See Gen. 22:1-19.)

This ram represented Christ, the Lamb of God without spot or blemish from whom the whole family of God is given. "Now, therefore, you are no more strangers and foreigners, but fellow citizens with the saints, and of the household of God" (Eph. 2:19).

Just as Jesus died that we might have His life and become His bride, we, too, are called upon to make sacrifices of self in order to make family work. "Husbands, love your wives, even as Christ also loved the church [assembly of called-out-ones], and gave Himself for it" (Eph. 5:25).

The covenant of family

Family is a power from God because it is based on covenant. God entered into covenant with Abraham saying, "I...will multiply you exceedingly...and you shall be a father of many nations." God changed Abram's name to Abraham which means "father of a multitude." This covenant had to do with family. This covenant was not only established between God and Abraham but between God and all of Abraham's descendants. "And I will establish My covenant between Me and you and your seed after you in their generations for an everlasting covenant to be a God unto you, and to your seed after you" (Gen. 17:2-7).

The promise of blessing

The blessings of Abraham were associated with the covenant of family. God blessed Abraham by giving his descendants a land—Canaan—as an everlasting covenant (Gen. 17:8). Canaan was the promised land of God. It was a land flowing with milk and honey (Lev. 20:24). Milk and honey are terms that represent the blessing of God that accompanied the covenant of God. The blessings of God are associated with God's covenant for family.

Abraham imparted the blessing to his son Isaac who imparted it to his son Jacob (who was also named Israel) who imparted it to his sons.

We who believe in God through Christ are the true heirs of Abraham according to Galatians 3:29: "And if you are Christ's, then you are Abraham's seed, and heirs according to the promise."

The blessings of God are associated with family when we are family as God intended. God bestows His blessing upon that which He appoints. He appointed, empowered, and bestowed His blessing upon family.

The blessings of family may produce wealth but have to do with far more than making money. A family can be relatively poor and still be blessed of God. We are blessed when we have good health, sound mind, food, shelter, clothing, peace, joy, and relationships. I feel blessed when I step into a warm shower to bathe or receive a letter from a special friend. To have family and be a part of family is a blessing in itself.

Blessings can come in very large or small portions. They can be any good thing that comes to anyone at any given time, family or not. The homeless man can count a warm meal at the rescue mission as a blessing, but he himself is not necessarily under the blessing. The person in great pain may count it a blessing to find relief in a pain pill, but that does not mean he or she is necessarily under the blessing.

The presence of God in the family empowers the family. The absence of God in the family leaves the family powerless. The empowered family is under the blessing while the powerless family struggles under the curse.

Families who stay bonded together in the name of Jesus will have bestowed upon them more abundant blessing.

Broken covenant

The break-up of family life is a breach of God's covenant with man. The second chapter of Malachi raises these questions: "Have we not all one Father? Has not one God created us? Why do we deal treacherously every man against his brother...?"

How did they deal treacherously with one another? Two ways: First, by profaning the covenant of their fathers (Mal. 2:10). As a nation, Judah broke covenant with God by marrying the heathens of the land and bowing down to their foreign gods (v.11).

Second, by dealing treacherously with the wives of their youth—their companions and wives by covenant. "Therefore take heed to your spirit, and let none deal treacherously against the wife of his youth. For the Lord, God of Israel, says that He hates putting away [divorce]..." (Mal. 2:15-16). God expects the dad to be faithful in his

24

covenant with God by being faithful in his covenant with his wife.

We break covenant with God when we fail to live responsibly as husbands and fathers. Breaking covenant with God is abandonment. We abandon His will in our lives and take away our family's spiritual covering. Moreover, we abandon ourselves because we cut ourselves off from the blessing that accompanies the covenant. It is the father, not the mother, as precious as mothers are, who pass on the fullness of the blessing from one generation to another. The dad will never find complete satisfaction until that covenant has been restored to him or he has sought and found forgiveness from God.

That may be discouraging to dads who already find themselves separated from their children. But take heart! "If we confess our sins, He is faithful and just to forgive us our sins, and to cleanse us from all unrighteousness" (1 John 1:9). Further passages from Malachi say, "'Return unto Me, and I will return unto you,' says the Lord of hosts....'And I will spare them, as a man spares his own son who serves him....But unto you who fear My name shall the Sun of righteousness arise with healing in His wings; and you shall go forth, and grow up as calves of the stall'" (Mal. 3:7, 17; 4:2).

The priority of family

Family, as God intends family, takes priority. We give priority to family by giving priority to meeting the needs of the individual members of the family.

The needs of each family member are unique. In the nurturing family situation, all of the members will feel special and as though they are given priority. We will be doing what is in the best interests of all when the best interest of any one is served.

The dad's main job is to preserve the family, preserve the idea of family, and preserve the power and blessing of family. The mother's job is to help him do that. The husband and wife who so live their lives are in covenant with God.

PROCESSING GUIDE

How did the absence or presence of God in your family of origin make a difference?

How could things have been different?

How does the absence or presence of God in your present family make a difference?

How could things be different?

What prevents those things from being different?

What new commitments are emerging within you?

Write your thoughts and feelings about the ideas presented in this chapter.

Chapter 4

THE DAD POWER

God placed the man as the head of his family. Paul writes, "But I would have you know that the head of every man is Christ; and the head of the woman is the man; and the head of Christ is God" (1 Cor. 11:3).

As the heads of our families, we men have been given a special empowerment from God to do our jobs as dads. Moms do not have this dad-empowerment and cannot get it. Brothers and sisters do not have it and cannot get it. Step-dads, uncles, aunts, and grandparents do not have it and cannot get it. Each of those have their own empowerment that corresponds with their function, but it is not *the dad* power.

The dad is a supernatural, transcendent power that flows from Father-God, enabling us, as men, to be godly fathers to our families. It is a deposit of God-life within us. Once we have been given this power from above, we are able to be what we are supposed to be in relationship to our families. When *the dad* is operating, *the dad* power is automatically present.

God's power

This empowerment is from God, therefore it transcends us. It is a supernatural, God-given empowerment that comes upon us dads which enables us to be more and do more than we ever could as mere men—that is what I am calling *the dad* power.

Power, as I am using it here, has to do with an unseen

27

energy or force that makes something work. In our case as men, it is that force with which God has gifted us that enables us to be what He wants us to be to our families. Without *the dad* power in operation, we men cannot be dads as God intended.

We have been given a power in particular that enables us to be more than bulls that sire offspring. We have a power that comes from God to operate according to the plan and purpose of God. He appointed, anointed, inspired, and empowered us to do *the dad.*

When *the dad* is present in power, we appear bigger than life to our families. Our wives feel safer and more secure in our presence, and our children brag to the other kids on the block, "My dad can whip your dad."

Knowing that this empowerment comes only from God leaves us weak and vulnerable before God.

God's authority

The dad power carries with it an authority that comes from God. God is the highest authority in the universe. He alone gives ultimate authority to people and angels. When we seek God's guidance and act accordingly, we will act under the power of His authority. Things are accomplished.

My three grandchildren had been playing in a bedroom when the fighting began. My son looked at me and said with confidence, "I'll take care of this."

He towered over the small children as he stood in the doorway of the room where they were playing. "Luke," he asked with a calm but authoritative voice, "What happened here? Why is Zachary crying?"

Luke gave his it-wasn't-my-fault defense.

Looking for verification, my son turned to his daughter, Cody, and asked, "What happened?"

She gave her version.

A stone-dead silence fell over the children as they awaited the verdict from Dad. I waited, too, expecting some punitive action. But without a word, Dad turned and walked away from them.

"What happened?" I asked.

He explained, "I paused and asked, 'Father, what am I to do with this?' The words came to me, 'Walk away from it.' So I walked away from it."

The issue was settled. Dad had sought God's wisdom, believed he had it, and acted on it. The children happily played with one another for the rest of the evening.

"Can you imagine," I said to my son, "what power we would walk in if we consulted God like that all the time?"

God's model

This God-given authority means that we will be a god-model whether we want to be or not. Whatever we are like, good or bad, is what our children will probably grow up thinking God is like.

Pat Springle wrote, "Our views of God, our self-concepts and our abilities to relate to others are primarily shaped by our parental relationships. If our parents were loving and supportive, we will probably believe that God is loving and strong. If, however, our parents were harsh and demanding, we will probably believe that God is impossible to please."[3]

Springle uses charts to help the reader understand how one's relationship with his father and mother may have shaped his relationship with God. I filled out the charts checking the boxes that best described my relationship with my dad, my mom, and then God. The choices were "always," "very often," "sometimes," "hardly ever," "never," or "don't know." These choices applied to a column of characteristics such as gentle, stern, loving, aloof, disapproving, distant, close and intimate.

I checked the "hardly ever" box for most of the characteristics on my dad page. He was neither gentle nor stern,

---

[3]Pat Springle, *Rapha's 12-Step Program for Overcoming Codependency* (Houston and Dallas: Rapha Publishing/Word 1991), 15.

kind nor angry, demanding nor supportive. He was not there to be any of those.

The check marks, however, were spread around on the mom page. She was gracious, never harsh; compassionate, never impatient; always just, hardly ever unpredictable. She was there in most of the ways that counted.

My God page looked like a duplicate copy of my mom page. She, as it turned out, shaped my view of God more than my dad. Nevertheless, I did not know the father characteristics as I now do.

If we are operating under *the dad* power, we will more likely represent God as He truly is to our children.

God's representative

We are not just the dads of our families, we are the dads of our families for God. God not only empowers us to be His representatives to our families, He empowers us to act for Him on behalf of our families.

I was in prayer one morning and found myself with outstretched arms, my palms downward, pronouncing a blessing over our children and their families. While doing this, I envisioned Jesus suspended in air, dressed in white, with his arms outstretched just as I had mine. I saw a man standing in front of Him, superimposed like a double exposure, and he had his arms outstretched as well. He was doing what the Lord was doing. He was blessing his family. Yet he was not blessing his family in and of himself; Jesus was blessing his family through him.

Afterwards, I felt confident God was using me to bless my family with His authority and power to provide a protective covering over them. I also felt God was revealing to me what *the dad* looks like in operation—Him working through us.

God's fathering

We need not concern ourselves about *our* ability to be *the dad*. We cannot. It is not about what we can do. It is about allowing God as Father to so invade our lives that it is Father-God doing the business of fathering through us. I call this exchanged fathering—borrowed from the idea of the exchanged life described by the apostle Paul in Galatians 2:20 which reads, "I am crucified with Christ: nevertheless I live; yet not I, but Christ lives in me: and the life which I now live in the flesh I live by the faith of the Son of God, who loved me, and gave Himself for me."

We need *the dad* of Father-God implanted within our being. We need more than to *do* like Him. We need His power to *be* like Him.

Our love for our family is God loving our family through us. Our service to our family is God serving our family through us. Our support for our family is God supporting our family through us. Our discipline of our children is God disciplining (discipling) our children through us. We are not asking God to bless our works. We are asking God to be our works. We are asking Him to invade our lives so entirely that we will be the presence and power of God to our family.

The dad is a sold-out, totally surrendered, Spirit-filled, Spirit-sensitive, Spirit-led man of God. He has God's love, joy, peace, patience, kindness, goodness, gentleness, meekness, mercy, grace, life, and power to pour out upon his family.

When my son consulted the Holy Spirit before taking his own punitive action with his children, he waited for God's response. God's response not only solved the problem, but made life easier for everyone involved. While listening to the Holy Spirit in that moment of time, my son traded his life for God's life, his will for God's will, his potential reaction to God's pro-action. It was a small, yet awesome demonstration of *the dad* power in operation.

As we so live our lives, we will bring honor, praise, and glory to His name. We are to live so surrendered to the lordship of Jesus Christ that when our family members look at us they will not see us, but they will see God in us.

It is not easy to walk in this kind of abandonment to the Father's life within us. It takes practice. It requires that we show as much mercy to ourselves as God would have us show toward others.

The exchanged life is a changed life. We are changed by God who is at work within us from the inside out. We cannot make that change happen on our own. Father God has to quicken to life *the dad* seed within every man of faith and cause that seed to mature, just as it is in the body of Christ, unto a "perfect man, to the measure of the stature of the fullness of Christ" (Eph. 4:13b).

God in Christ is the "everlasting Father" of us all (Is. 9:6). He is father by nature and fathers us all directly. Nevertheless, He has chosen *the dad* within the man to live out His Fatherhood in the families of men as far as that is possible and available. Father-God is THE DAD of *the dad* within the man.

PROCESSING GUIDE

How has your perception of God been framed by the authority of your parents, especially your dad?

How are you as a dad framing your children's perception of God?

How might you change in order to better model God?

Ask God to begin showing you who He really is as Father and to impart *the dad* power to you.

Write your thoughts and feelings about the ideas presented in this chapter.

Chapter 5

THE WAR AGAINST FAMILY

Margie stood up to testify: "On September 25th, 1980, my husband walked out on our family of four kids." We wonder: Dad, where did you go? Why did you go? Did you get entangled in the web of sexual sin? Did you drown in a bottle of booze? Did you cave in under the weight of financial responsibility? Or did the grass just look greener on the other side? Dad probably doesn't know for sure himself. He and his family are casualties of a vicious war that is being waged in the spirit world against family.

Family is the eternal will of God. All of the works of God, especially the redeeming work of Christ on the cross, are aspects of God's plan to purchase a family for Himself. Every word He sends, every sign and wonder He performs, every deed He accomplishes are sub-steps toward achieving His eternal goal. Nothing will stop God from having what He has already paid for.

Satan will try anyway. His main intention in all eternity is to thwart the will of God by destroying family. Surely he knows that family is God's eternal plan and purpose. He knows that God's power and blessing are upon family. If he can destroy the family, he can break the covenant, cut off the power, and rob us of the blessing.

He is out to destroy family any way he can: through war, famine, poverty, crime, divorce, feminism, addictions, and especially lust and sexual sins (fornication, adultery, homosexuality, pornography, pedophilia, bestiality, etc.).

33

While sin is sin, sexual sins can be more devastating to family than any other. Family is based on the sexual relationship of a man and a woman who have become one flesh. If Satan can destroy that, he has destroyed the integrity of the marriage and violated the sanctity of family. He has cut off the power of family.

Family has suffered a great loss as a result of the sexual revolution of the sixties. "Free sex" has turned out to be very costly with the high rise of illegitimacy, sexual addictions, sexual abuses, and AIDS. We have generated an amoral society. People are flaunting their sexual preferences in public and mocking God. Their lack of repentance looks much like the apostle Paul's description in Romans 1:24-28: "God also gave them up to uncleanness through the lusts of their own hearts, to dishonor their own bodies between themselves: who changed the truth of God into a lie, and worshipped and served the creature more than the Creator...For this cause God gave them up unto vile affections: for even their women did change the natural use into that which is against nature: And likewise also the men, leaving the natural use of the woman, burned in their lust one toward another; men with men working that which is unseemly, and receiving in themselves that recompense [penalty] of their error....God gave them over to a reprobate mind..."

In order to promote his anti-family agenda, Satan has engaged himself in politics, science, education, media, music, entertainment, religion, and every other aspect of society. The anti-family agenda is in keeping with the spirit of the anti-Christ that has been loosed in the world today.

By waging war against the souls of men, Satan can destroy family—thereby trashing the birthright with the blessing. The birthright and the blessing can be lost in one generation. It is like passing a baton in a relay race from one runner to another. If that baton is dropped, the race is lost. One generation of absentee dads has resulted in a lost generation of kids. Failure to pass on the birthright and the blessing leaves the family vulnerable to the curse. This curse is then passed on from generation to generation unless God shows mercy and reestablishes the authority of the dad in our homes.

We need to clearly understand who the enemy is, what his tactics are, and why he is hell-bound to destroy the family through spiritual decapitation. Satan has had too much success in wrecking family life during the past few decades.

Abandonment

A fatherless family is a decapitated family. By decapitated family, I mean a family from whom the spiritual head, the husband and dad, has been removed. It is a severed, damaged, and potentially cursed family. Children who grow up in a severed family are victims of abandonment, and abandonment is abuse. This kind of abandonment has reached epidemic proportions in our western society today, especially in the U. S.

We dads are quicker to abandon the family than the moms. We either split, or we are there in body only. We abandon our moral, social, spiritual, physical, relational, and economic responsibilities. Since these are our responsibilities, they go unfulfilled. Many moms have been left behind to do the best they can, but it is not their function to be what only the dad is given to be and do.

Moms can instill moral and spiritual values in their children to some degree, but it will usually carry a different weight from that of the dad. The mom influence is different from the dad influence. Moms do not have the same power. Children need what both parents are empowered to give.

The absence of dad, therefore, has resulted in a moral, social, spiritual, and economic decay in our society today. Family is the stitching that binds the fabric of society together. It is the power of a strong and thriving society.

When the family breaks down, society follows. Societal decay is happening in America today.

Our children are birthing children. Children are killing other children. Children are in rebellion to their parents. Children are using drugs, alcohol, and having sex at younger than ever ages.

Gangs are often formed in order to provide social safety and structure that is otherwise missing in their world. Parents are selling their babies for booze and drugs. Welfare has become a dead-end street for countless numbers of people. Loss of income and homelessness is rising.

Children of abandonment suffer a loss they cannot understand. The loss that is sustained from the father who is taken in an accident, fatal illness, war, or some other catastrophe is different from the loss that is felt when dad is taken away by self-centeredness, alcoholism, drug addiction, crime, workaholism, domestic violence, divorce, and adultery. Fathers who leave without warning or without preparing their children devastate their children. Yet, there can never be enough preparation for this father deficit in the family.

The loss that is felt within the abandoned individual often turns to anger and rage which is expressed or suppressed in many different disguises. The child is raised in a dysfunctional family system, suffering pain which is often medicated with alcohol, drugs, sex, or other destructive, obsessive-compulsive behaviors.

A lost generation

We are living in a lost generation. Our children today are referred to as Generation X. Some say America is now living in the post-Christian era. What has happened to us? ...Dad went away.

The 1994 Census Bureau released information in 1996 declaring that over 27 million children (38%) under the age of 18 in the United States live apart from their biological fathers. Most of the men in prison today grew up without fathers in their lives. Not only do growing numbers of children live without their dads in the home, but many of those children do not see their fathers in a typical year.

Myron Magnet painted the grim statistical picture for us in a 1992 Fortune magazine article. "Over half of all first marriages now end in divorce," Magnet wrote. Of these, 57% had children under 18 years of age. "Over a million kids a year have to weather the breakup of their parents' marriage. An epidemic rise of out-of-wedlock births—from under 4% of children born in 1950 to a startling 27% in 1989—has further swollen the number of children in single-parent families. Two of every three black children are born out of wedlock today, and one of every five white children...A quarter of American children live in single-parent, usually female-headed, households."[4]

Many experts believe that big government, the great society, and the welfare programs provide incentive to have children out of wedlock. Liberal news media have mocked and scorned those who have spoken out in favor of family values. The gay rights agenda stresses the preeminence of the individual over the family.

Divorce and illegitimacy teaches the next generation what the family game plan is. Some children cannot see themselves with a partner for life.

David Blankenhorn, founder and president of the Institute for American Values, warns that "fatherlessness is the most harmful demography trend of this generation. It is the leading cause of declining child well-being in our society. It is also the engine driving our most urgent social problems, from crime to adolescent pregnancy to child sexual abuse to domestic violence against women."[5]

Ken Canfield of the National Center for Fathering has

---

[4]Myron Magnet, "The American Family," *Fortune*, 10 August 1992, 42-43.
[5]David Blankenhorn, *Fatherless America* (New York: Harper Collins Publishers, Harpers Perennial, 1995), 1.

gathered information reporting that children who grow up in fatherless homes are more likely to "be absent from school, perform less well on standardized tests and school assignments, drop out of high school, be sexually active, be susceptible to peer pressure, be depressed and/or show aggressive behavior (especially girls), [and] be susceptible to disease. As adults, the chances are greater that those raised without a father will: suffer from poverty, receive welfare, marry earlier, have children out of wedlock, divorce, commit delinquent acts, [and] engage in drug or alcohol use."[6] I would also suggest that they are more likely to turn to occult practices and religious cults in search of meaning, identity, and power.

Canfield cites another 1990 report showing that children with highly involved fathers are "more confident and less anxious when placed in unfamiliar settings, better able to deal with frustration, better able to adapt to changing circumstances and breaks from their routine, [and] better able to gain a sense of independence and an identity outside the mother/child relationship."[7] He adds that "a 1990 study found that the greatest predictor of whether a child would grow into an adult demonstrating 'empathetic concern' (love) as a 31-year-old, was whether their father was involved in child care."[8] Then, citing a paper by Harris and Furstenberg, he writes: "Fathers who spend time with their children as adolescents 'promote educational and economic achievement,' and fathers who maintain a close and stable emotional bond with their adolescents protect them from engaging in delinquent

---

[6]Canfield, Ken. "The Importance of Fathers," National Center for Fathering, January 1997, citing Sara McLanahan and K. Booth, "Mother-only families: problems, prospects and politics," *Journal of Marriage and Family* S1 (1989): 557:580. For resources see: http:\\www.fathers.com

[7]Ibid., citing Carla Cantor, "The father factor," *Working Mother*, June 1991, 39-43.

[8]Ibid., citing E. M. Koestner and P.D. Fairweather, "The family of origin of empathetic concern; a 26-year longitudinal study," *Journal of Personality and Social Psychological*, 58(4) (1990): 709-717.

behavior."[9]

Values have to be taught. Our children are going to learn values, good or bad. They learn primarily from what they see, hear, and experience in the home. If they are not taught good values in the traditional institutions of the home, church, and school, they will learn other values on the streets from anyone who will teach them.

Media role

Hollywood and liberal TV can be blamed for the devaluation of the family through the blatant use of violence, foul language, immoral sex, the occult, the display of anti-Christian sentiment in their programming, and in their consent to alternative lifestyles.

Men on TV are most often portrayed as gross, insensitive, macho, vulgar, immoral, unfaithful, irresponsible, buffoons, or wimps. Many programs and commercials appeal to a man's ego to have a faster car, a sexier woman, and an uninhibited lifestyle. There are precious few sitcoms that represent an intact nuclear family that is also healthy according to Biblical standards. Our models have vanished.

Media contends that they are only reflecting the way things are. Many of us, however, contend that media has much to do with making things the way they are. When one city block of bad "Hollywood" kids is portrayed as typical in Small Town, USA, it serves to suggest to kids everywhere that this way of life is not only acceptable but desirable.

Absence of strong male models

Even secular social scientists are now admitting that many of our social problems today stem from the absence

---

[9]Ibid., citing Kathleen M. Harris, Frank Furstenberg, Jr., and Jeremy Marmer, "Paternal involvement with adolescents in intact families: the influence of father over the life course" (paper presented at the annual meeting of the American Sociological Association, New York, N.Y., August 16-20, 1996).

of a strong male father figure in the home. When dads abandoned their responsibilities as fathers, they cut off the power of *the dad* from being passed on to their sons. Boys grow up not knowing how to be husbands and dads.

Something of the wife and mom nature is missing in the daughters when a strong, loving, caring, sensitive, giving, and responsible dad is absent from the home. These daughters are less likely to distinguish the difference that a mom and a dad make, thus their own sexuality becomes clouded.

Children grow up in these severed homes, get married out of lust, and have little idea what true love and marriage looks like. No amount of pre-marital counseling sessions can put into a couple what they should have been taught all through their formative years. They are less likely to know what marriage is all about. They are not prepared or trained for it. Consequently, they get married for all of the wrong reasons. The marriage does not work, they divorce, and the children are lost to abandonment.

Abandoned people abandon people

Paul, mulling over the absence of close friends in his life, asked his wife, Rebecca, "Do you think we've abandoned people?"

She was unsure at first but remembered some former relationships, and answered, "We did not mean to, but there are some people who I believe have felt abandoned by us."

"I have to admit," Paul said, "that I can see a pattern of inviting people into our lives, getting involved with them for a short period of time, and then, for various reasons, distancing ourselves from them. I wonder if that tendency has to do with my father deserting me. Only in recent years have I realized just how much that affected me—how lonely and lost I've felt because of it."

He reflected on those thoughts for a moment, then asked, "Do you think abandoned people abandon people?"

I believe the answer is "yes." We often learn patterns of behavior by how the significant others in our lives treated us as children.

If we are the victims of abandonment, we are going to have feelings of abandonment. We will most likely become perpetrators of abandonment. We will most likely be attracted to other abandoned victims who have also become perpetrators of abandonment and get into relationships with them. We will most likely set ourselves up to be abandoned by them and set them up to be abandoned by us. We want to learn to do differently.

Abandonment is a spiritual issue

We are in relationships with mates, parents, children, neighbors, fellow Christians, co-workers, and many others in life. These relationships exist to meet essential needs among us. Different people meet different needs.

These needs touch on every life area—things such as good nutrition, a sanitary environment, shelter, clothing, proper hygiene, education, love, hugs, encouragement, validation, safety, purpose, significance, authenticity, eligibility, hope, dignity, and power. It will be our responsibility as dads to meet many of these needs.

Many of these responsibilities are God-given. When we abandon any of these relationships, we have not only abandoned our responsibilities to ourselves and others, but we have abandoned God's call on us as well. Abandonment, therefore, becomes a spiritual issue.

Abandonment creates losses. Many of these losses cannot be regained. When we are the victims of abandonment and its subsequent losses, we must learn how to grieve these losses and surrender them to God. In so doing, we can ultimately resolve them and get on with our lives.[10]

Abandonment is the disease of family which is caused

---

[10]An excellent exercise for dealing with losses is found in *Boundary Power*, a book which I wrote with Mike S. O'Neil. See Chapter 14: "Resolving the Losses" (Power Life Resources, P. O. Box 110512, Nashville, TN 37222; phone 615-361-0691; www.powerliferesources.com).

by the absence of *the dad*. Therefore, the cure lies in the restoration of *the dad* to the family.

PROCESSING GUIDE

What particular weapons has Satan used in trying to destroy your family of origin?

Which, if any, of those weapons are present in your family situation now?

How did you experience abandonment as a child growing up?

How have you abandoned others, especially the members of your own family?

Write your thoughts and feelings about the ideas presented in this chapter.

Chapter 6

HEALING THE FATHER-WOUND

George, nervously fidgeting with the coins in his pocket, ambled up to me after the support group meeting and asked if I would be his mentor. "Sure," I answered. After all, I had a head full of gray hair and he was young enough to be my son.

After meeting for lunch a couple of times, I soon realized that he was needing more than a mentor. He was looking for a dad. He was starving for the affection his non-responsive dad failed to give him during his formative years.

He needed his dad to affirm him and give him an identity. We all need that. "This crippling 'father-wound,' which men have suffered for generations, is a wound of absence," writes Gordon Dalby.[11] Failure to get affirmation and identity from dad is a type of abandonment—abandonment of responsibility. It leaves us wondering, Who am I? Whose am I? This abandonment is a violation against our character and emotions.

I sat across the table from George and watched him sip on cocktails to medicate the shame of his more gripping addiction: homosexuality. He was looking for his dad in older men. He hated that about himself. He knew his answer was not in the bottle or in other men, but he was powerless to stop this self-destructive behavior. He needed healing from the father-wound.

---

[11]Gordon Dalby, *Fight Like a Man* (Wheaton: Tyndale House Publishers 1995), viii.

George's abandonment wounds made it difficult for him to enter into healthy and nurturing relationships. He went from one bad relationship to another. Abandoned people are drawn to other abandoned people from whom they hope to get validation, but from whom they get more abandonment.

Since the father-wound is caused from abandonment which results in a lack of validation and identification, then the healing from this wound has to come from a father-figure who has the authority and power to validate and give identity; namely our fathers. The healing comes from knowing who we are because we know whose we are.

If we were not validated as a child, Father-God is the only source of validation in adulthood. "Only Jesus," writes Dalby, "can heal the father-wound, because only he can overcome our sin-nature and restore relationship with the true and present Father of all men."[12] We need for God to sovereignly heal our father-wounds and restore our relationships. He does this by making us His sons. Dalby: "Only the dignity of sonship can overcome the shame of abandonment."[13] What a profound statement.

In order to promote healing and restoration, we want to cooperate with the Holy Spirit in three time frames: We need to change the present, deal with the past, and build toward the future. This chapter identifies the steps that are needed to change the present and deal with the past. The remaining chapters build toward the future of godly fathering.

Humility: recognizing the problem

The first step we can take toward healing and restoration is to recognize that we have an abandonment problem. We want to unmask the pride behind which we hide our insecurities. "God resists the proud, but gives grace to the humble" (Jas. 4:6).

---

[12]Ibid., ix.
[13]Ibid., ix.

Most of us have sheltered our feelings so completely that we fail to see we have a problem. We are so ashamed of ourselves and our feelings that we pass blame on to others. This blaming game was perfected in the garden of Eden when Adam spoke those immortal words, "The woman You gave to be with me, she gave me of the tree, and I ate it" (Gen. 3:12).

Humility is honesty—the ability to own the truth about ourselves. Arrogance, haughtiness, and blaming pale in the light of how wretched we are without Jesus. Humility is coming out of denial into reality.

My daddy lay stone cold dead in the casket. People paraded past his body, then turned to console the members of the family. I do not remember if others were grieving. I wasn't. I didn't feel good or bad about him dying. I only remember having a good time talking and kidding around with my friends. I was fourteen years old.

Forty-two years later. It was my time to share. The guys in my group couldn't believe that I was not angry over my dad issues. "Dad issues?" I questioned. "What dad issues? I don't have any dad issues. I don't feel angry. I don't feel glad. I don't feel anything. Can't you see? He was not in my life enough to feel anything about him one way or the other."

I did not know then that those "nothing" feelings were my dad issues. I should have had some kind of feeling. But I had frozen the rage of abandonment deep inside of me. It was only when the Holy Spirit began to heal me of it that I learned I had a father-wound. He brought me to humility.

Recognizing abandonment as sin

The second step toward healing and restoration is to recognize that abandonment is sin.

Jesus said, "For if you forgive men their trespasses, your heavenly Father will also forgive you" (Matt. 6:14). Sin is a trespass. As such, it is a boundary violation. A boundary violation is anything that crosses a line of safety in our lives whether physically, spiritually, psychologically, emotionally, sexually, financially, or relationally. When that line is crossed, a violation occurs. All boundary violations are abusive. We violate God by trespassing His word and will, we violate others by trespassing their wills or our responsibilities toward them, and we violate ourselves by various abuses to ourselves. Violations can be as obvious as rape or as subtle as that of a non-respondent dad.

George's dad violated him when he failed to cuddle him in his lap and fill his little cup with love. George did not get it; therefore, he could not give it. We will have greater incentive to correct our bad behaviors if we recognize how devastating is the sin of abandonment.

Confessing the sin of abandonment

The third step toward healing and restoration is to recognize how we have abandoned others. "Confess your faults one to another, and pray one for another, that you may be healed" (Jas. 5:16).

Having owned abandonment as a sin, we need to obey the scriptures and confess it to others. Two good reasons for doing so: first, it brings the darkness of that sin out into the open for the light of Christ to eradicate it. "All things that are reproved [rebuked] are made manifest [visible] by the light: for whatsoever is made manifest [visible] is light" (Eph. 5:13). This verse indicates that the light of Christ turns darkness into light. Second, confessing our sins of abandonment holds us accountable to others.

We want to confess how we have been the victims of abandonment and the effect that has had upon us, and how we have abandoned others and what effect that has had upon them.

Repenting from the sin of abandonment

The fourth step to healing and restoration is to repent of abandonment, since we have recognized that it is a sin.

We approach this from two angles: We want to repent of the resentments we hold and the self-destructive behaviors we practice as victims of abandonment. We can let go of these bad feelings and behaviors much easier once we realize they are connected to abandonment. The second angle is to repent of our continual abandonment of others.

Repentance is regretting our past conduct enough to do something different with our lives, to change our minds and behaviors. Repentance cleans the house of our souls. Any charges against us that are dropped by others may depend largely upon how swept clean our own houses are.

God grants us repentance. When the Holy Spirit first fell upon the Gentiles, Peter explained that it was God who had also granted them repentance to life (Acts 11:18). In the early years of my walk with the Lord, He convicted me that I needed to repent of a certain sin in my life.

"OK, Lord, I repent." I had the words but not the heart for it.

"Repent!" He said repeatedly to me over the months. Each time I tried as best I could to white-knuckle my way out of that sin. Each time I fell flat on my face.

God, in His timing, used a circumstance in my life to expose that sin in order to produce godly sorrow and true repentance.

More often than not, I have experienced God's repentance process this way: He calls me to repent. I try. I fail. He calls again. I try and try again. I fail and fail and fail again. Then, He is faithful to bring me to the end of that sin, and I truly repent, not in my own strength, but because He granted repentance out of His mercy and grace toward me. We need, now, for God to bring us to godly sorrow in this matter of abandonment.

Forgiving others
The fifth step to healing and restoration is to forgive those who have harmed us. Tremendous healing is released through the forgiveness process.

Forgiving others of their trespasses against us is our business. Whether or not the other persons ask for that forgiveness is none of our business. We forgive others for our own sakes, because unforgiveness can lead to a root of bitterness, and a root of bitterness can lead to personal, physical, emotional, and spiritual problems. We need to do whatever it takes to liberate other persons from our resentments so we can be free from our resentments.

For the purposes of this study, we want to be alert to our need to forgive those who have abandoned us. If we are the sons of parental abandonment, we need to find it in our hearts to forgive our parents.

Financial problems, parental arguments, and a breakdown in communication were among the things that drove Alex to run away from home several times and adopt an alternative lifestyle. While at a Christian music festival, he accepted the Lord into his heart.

Months later, Alex and his dad attended a Christian revival meeting together. The invitation was given for people to come forward for prayer and ministry. Alex went up because he felt guilt encircling him. As he stood there crying his heart out and trying to figure out what in his life he needed to release, he felt a hand on his shoulder and heard a sniffle behind him. He thought, "That's my dad." He turned around and saw his dad weeping.

"OK, Lord," Alex muttered under his breath, "what am I supposed to do here?" Immediately he had a vision of a large cross with the words written over it, "Forgive him." The cross represented Alex's need to lay down his pride, anger, and resentments so he could ask for forgiveness. He also knew that his dad was a changed man and that he was to forgive him for everything in the past.

"I chose to forgive him," he testified. "We cried on each other's shoulders close to half an hour. Since then," he said, "we have had the intimate relationship a father and son should."

Alex knew in his heart that if he could forgive his dad,

the bitterness inside of him would be gone, and he would be able to forgive anyone.

Unforgiveness is like holding a debt against someone. "You owe me." Forgiveness is allowing that debt to be expunged from the ledger. It may help us to make an actual list of what we think dad owes us. Then, go down through that list and mark PAID by each item. Is that not what Jesus did for us? I love the words to the chorus, "I owed a debt I could not pay. He [Jesus] paid a debt He did not owe. I needed someone to wash my sins away..."

We strive for reconciliation in all strained relationships. Reconciliation disarms the unseen enemy in the war against family. However, forgiving an abusive person does not mean we have to go back into the abuse. It only means we can be free.

Asking forgiveness and making amends

The sixth step to healing and restoration is to ask for forgiveness from those we have harmed. If we have abandoned our children or step-children emotionally, spiritually, socially, or physically, we need to seek their forgiveness and make amends where possible.

Much more work is involved in securing forgiveness from others than in forgiving others. We want to be sure that we have done all within our power to secure their forgiveness. Jesus taught, "If you bring your gift to the altar, and there remember that your brother has ought against you, leave your gift there before the altar, and go your way; first be reconciled to your brother, and then come and offer your gift" (Matt. 5:23-24). We do what we can; yet, we face the fact that not everyone will forgive us and be reconciled to us.

Several sub-steps are involved in securing forgiveness from others. First, we want to make sure that we are changed persons, that we no longer do those things that bring injury to others. Showing others that we have truly repented goes a long way toward building trust. Second, we want to inventory the exact nature of our offenses to others and confess those. Third, we want to express sincere sorrow to our victims—show that we, in fact, hurt for them, that we feel their pain. If we do not truly feel their pain, we want to ask the Holy Spirit to touch us where we need to be touched. Fourth, we want to make restitution as far as possible for the offenses. Fifth, having done these things first, we are in a better position to ask for forgiveness in sincerity.

Making restitution can be most difficult. We can pay back money we stole from our employer. We can fix the damage we did to our neighbor's fence. But how do we pay the debt for violating a child? How do we make up for those many years lost to abandonment? How do we remove the cloud of loneliness, fear, and rage that caused our own children to turn to drugs, alcohol, sex, or destructive relationships? How can we go back and fill those empty coffers?

Making amends and restitution may involve years of work to rebuild shattered lives. Wild seed, once sown, is difficult to weed. Nevertheless, we do whatever it takes to begin the process, to reverse the curse, to put to death those reasons that keep resentment alive. We may need to receive counseling for ourselves. We may need to provide counseling for them or offer to go to counseling with them. Abandonment takes something away from us; restitution hopes to give it back.

Forgiveness brings closure to unfinished business in our lives. Sometimes we have to go back to that unfinished business so we can go through it in order to get past it.

The healing for me

This book was started during a six-month period of time that I call my "people fast." It had to do with the Lord's work in delivering me from unhealthy caretaking of other people. I had no idea at the beginning of that fast that God would be healing me of dad issues.

"Lord," I asked a few months later, "this is the last day of my people fast. What do You have to say to me about that?" His answer profoundly changed my life:

"You will discover in time, as you have already suspected, that the caretaking was part of a cycle that led to your masculinity issues. You had not known how to be a man because you were raised by a woman. But that has all changed. You are now a man, My man. You are a man after My heart. You are a man who seeks My will, one who is willing to lay down all of who you are that I might have My complete will and way in your life. You are a man among men. You will be seen as a man's man, a father among the sons."

It was overwhelming to have my heavenly Father validate my manhood this way, saying in essence, "You are My beloved son [with a little "s"] in whom I am well pleased."

Moments later the Holy Spirit surprised me by permitting me to know intuitively that my dad was there with Him in heaven. I did not have assurance of that previously. "He deeply regretted the abandonment," the Holy Spirit said, "but understands that My grace is sufficient."

It was enough just to know that Dad was with the Lord. But He continued, "You will all be together in My glory. Your Dad knows who you are and is deeply pleased with who you have become. Just as it is with your son, you are a son who makes a father proud."

Those few but powerful words, spoken in God's perfect timing, healed me of my father-wound. I cannot tell you how comforting it was for the Lord to assure me that Dad was with Him and that he regretted the abandonment. I needed to know that.

I wept and told him, "Dad, I forgive you. I miss you and I love you. I wish that we could have had the father-son experience that I have with my son." (I cherish my relationships with my daughters. But I was a son in need of a father, and I was looking at this from the father-son point of view.)

This unique experience put closure on a spiritually surgical procedure that only God could perform with such precision and healing. God had already healed the father-wound between my son and me; this day he healed it between my dad and me. While healing is an on-going process between my children, stepchildren, and me, it is at least going on. God is still in the process of calling forth *the dad* within this man.

Ultimate healing and restoration will come as we are conformed more and more into the image of Jesus who imparts *the dad* within us. He makes us to be what we need to be for our loved ones.

PROCESSING GUIDE

Your answers to the following questions may help you determine if there is a pattern of abandonment in your life:

Make a list of those you feel have abandoned you in your life one way or another.

How has each one abandoned you?

What legitimate expectations should you have had of each of them?

What false expectations might you have had of each of them?

What reasons, if any, were given for the abandonment?

How might your life be different had each of them not abandoned you?

Have you been in and out of numerous relationships throughout your life?

If so, with whom?

What was the type of relationship you had with each of those? (mate, parent, church members, work peers, etc.)

Why did you abandon any of them?

How might your life be different had you not abandoned each of them?

If there has been a pattern of abandonment in your life, answer the following:

What amends or restitution do you need to make to your family members for your abandonment of them?

What resentments and unforgiveness do you have toward your dad?

"Unforgiveness," I wrote, "is like holding a debt against someone. 'You owe me.'" I suggested that it "may help us to make an actual list of what we think dad owes us."

If you are ready, make such a list now.

If you are ready, mark each item PAID.

Write your thoughts and feelings about the ideas presented in this chapter.

Chapter 7

MEETING FATHER-GOD

On April 4, 1978, my wife and I were radically converted. We needed to be. I had become a professed atheist. She admitted to being an agnostic. I did not believe that there was a god, spirit world, or an afterlife. "This earthly life is our one shot at it," I used to boast. "If you make a success of your life, pat yourself on the back. If you don't, kick yourself on the backside." I considered myself to be my own god.

I wallowed in that arrogance for a number of years which culminated in a brief encounter with the occult. That changed our lives. We didn't call it "occult" at that time. That probably would have turned me off. We were told it was psychic phenomenon. That was more intellectually appealing, and, you must understand, we thought we were very intellectual.

After some terrifying experiences, we went for prayer and received deliverance from those demonic powers that we had engaged. We soon learned through good Bible teaching that there are two kingdoms in the spirit realm. We had wandered into the wrong one. There is the kingdom of God with Jesus Christ as the King of kings, and there is the kingdom of darkness with Satan as the ruler of this world.

On that glorious day of our conversion, it was for me as though the veil of the temple of God was opened, and I saw through to the Holy of Holies. I knew beyond a shadow of a doubt that Jesus was alive and real and that I had been a genuine fool.

Needless to say, I repented that day. So did my wife. We decided to surrender our hearts and lives over to the complete will of God in Christ. We became something within ourselves that was different from the way we were before. We had no way of changing ourselves that way. We were literally translated from the kingdom of darkness to the Kingdom of God's light.

On that day in April, I met my heavenly Father-God. I didn't know much about Him as Father at that time. I first came to know Him as someone who loved me and took me just as I was. That was good enough for me.

The following years were spent in what I call my wilderness journey where He, through the power of His Holy Spirit, led me through His process of separating me from the world, sin, the power of the flesh, and the domain of Satan.

It was not until I began this book that God revealed the deeper aspects of His fatherhood to me. Until then, I knew Jesus as my savior, lord, shepherd, and big brother; and I knew the Holy Spirit as my teacher, comforter, cleanser, and guide. I knew God called Himself our Father, but I did not fully appreciate the reality of that.

He continues to reveal His nature as Father to me. The more I come to know Him that way, the more I become the kind of father He is. I am taking on His character.

Knowledge of the Father

Father-God revealed His Son in order that His Son might reveal Him as Father. God revealed this Father-Son relationship as an example, even prototype, of what He wants between Himself and us. He wants many sons brought to glory. "For it became Him, for whom are all things, and by whom are all things, *in bringing many sons unto glory*, to make the captain of their salvation perfect through sufferings" (Heb. 2:10).

God revealed Himself in Jesus Christ to make His intentions known to us; that is, He wants a family for Himself, a body and a bride for His Son, and a temple for His Holy Spirit. These are all very personal and intimate terms God has used to describe how He wants to be in relationship with us.

We do not meet Father-God just so we can have a one-time religious experience whereupon we get a free ticket to heaven. We do not meet Him just so we can have someone to whine at when we get a little mud on our faces. We do not meet Him just so He can play Santa Claus in time of need. We meet Him in order to develop an abiding, intimate relationship with Him.

The heart of Father-God

God wants more than our just knowing *about* Him. He wants us to *know* Him personally. He wants us to know His heart. A sweeping review of the scriptures highlight the heart of Father-God:

He blesses His people. He pronounces His blessings upon persons. He is faithful. He promises to never leave us or forsake us. He keeps His promises. He cares for us and watches over us. He shepherds us, protects us, and provides for us. He has compassion upon us. He shows mercy and forgiveness. He draws near to us when we draw near to Him. He loves us, saves us, and delivers us from evil. He exalts and rewards us. He overshadows us. He is patient. He is good toward us. He is gracious and gives us grace. He keeps us. He is a God of peace. He is truth. He strengthens us. He rejoices over us. He is our healer. Because of His great love for us, He disciplines us as sons. He is jealous when we are unfaithful and angry when we are defiant and rebellious.

Father-God gave us Jesus who is our redeemer, justifier, substitute, righteousness, salvation, and glorifier. He is the author and finisher of our faith, the apostle and high priest of our calling, shepherd and guardian of our souls. He is our advocate, the author of eternal salvation, the bread of life, our deliverer, the good shepherd, the way, the truth, life, and light. He is the mediator between us and the Father and is always interceding for us.

Jesus gave us the Holy Spirit to be His abiding presence within us; to give us the power of His lordship; to lead us, teach us, comfort us, and help us.

Through Christ and the Holy Spirit we are a new creation, the righteousness of God in Christ, the body of Christ, the bride of Christ, God's family, God's flock, His habitation, His spiritual house, His temple, children of God, chosen ones, the elect, heirs, lights, sons of God, trees of righteousness, vessels of honor, vessels of mercy, the pillar and ground of truth, the New Jerusalem. That is as Father-God wants it. "'For I know the plans that I have for you,' declares the Lord, 'plans for welfare and not for calamity to give you a future and a hope'" (Jer. 29:11 NAS).

Intimacy with the Father

God not only wants us to know Him, He wants to be friends with us. Imagine that! You and me—personal buddies with the highest authority in all the universe! Jesus told His followers, "Henceforth I do not call you servants; for the servant does not know what his lord does: but I have called you friends; for all things that I have heard of My Father I have made known unto you" (John 15:15).

The writing below, which came shortly after my conversion in 1978, called me into a more intimate relationship with God as my heavenly Father. I pray that you may hear God's voice calling you to a closer walk with Him.

Will you walk with Me and talk with Me as though I were the only one?

When you have brotherly love toward someone, you feel affection toward them; you want to be with them, talk with them, do things together. I love you, My people, and I want to be your friend. I want to spend time with you and hold you and talk with you.

I hunger for your fellowship. I am jealous when your heart is turned toward another love. Your attention is here and there and everywhere, but not on Me. You do not love Me with brotherly love yet. For that love compels you to want to fellowship with Me.

Desire, My people, to be My friend, for I am already your friend. Desire to love Me with brotherly love, and I will give you that affection by which to love Me.

Have I not said in My word, have I not promised you that whatsoever things you ask of Me I will give to you if you abide in My word? Ask of Me what I ask of you to ask, and surely I will give it to you.

"You shall love the Lord your God with all your heart, soul, mind, and strength." Ask Me to show you what it means to love Me that way, and I will anxiously show you. For My heart is empty for you to love Me this way. This is the purpose for which I made you and redeemed you with My blood. There is no other legitimate purpose for your life. All else that you do in this life is secondary and of naught if first you do not love Me with all your heart, soul, mind, and strength. I am the Lord your God who made you, who formed you for this very purpose.

Do not be deceived by the world or by the lust of the flesh. These things will pass away, but My word is forever. If you do not abide in My word, you have no part in Me nor I in you. Do not be deceived My little ones; the time is short and the moments are precious. Soon we will be together as one for all eternity, but for now our fellowship is one in Spirit and truth. Follow after My Spirit and I will impart My truth.

As we walk down life's pathway side by side, there is no other one besides Me. I am your only true love. I have things to say to you, things to show you, places in the spirit to take you; but I cannot if you are not listening to Me and fellowshipping with Me and turning to Me with all your heart, soul, mind, and strength.

I will pour out My Spirit on those who diligently seek Me and follow after Me, who are willing to be invisible, who have no part in self-abasement and recognition but who will empty themselves of self and follow after Me with a whole heart.

Do not delay to search for Me, My people. I am at your door this very hour, waiting and knocking to come in with you, to sup with you. To sup with you is My way of saying I want fellowship with you as I had with Moses when two men would talk with one another as the closest of friends.

Oh, how I want to be your friend as you are to Me. How I long to hold your hand and walk through an autumn woods with you, strolling together, as it were, kicking up the fallen leaves. I want to be as near to you every moment of your life as the warm summer breeze is upon your brow.

Reach out to Me, My beloved; I am waiting right in front of you to take your hand and lead you on. We have a mountain to climb together, you and I; and that climb is as individual as that—you and I, together, hand in hand.

Do not delay, My children. There is not time for foolishness, for folly. There is not time to waste on the worries and cares of this world. Oh, if only you knew the things I have in store for you. You would not hesitate a moment to drop everything and rush into My arms. Not because of the "things," but because of My love.

Come to Me. Come to Me. Come to Me.
Dine with Me and I with you.
The feast is ready.
The call goes forth. Do not delay.
Come, My precious ones. Come.
I am waiting for you.

You must be born again

Before we can have this kind of intimacy, before we can take on His character, before *the dad* can come forth within us, before we can ever really have family restored to us the way God intended family, we must have the Spirit of God dwelling within us. We must be born into the family of God and make Jesus the lord of our lives.

Jesus told Nicodemus that unless one is born again, he cannot see and enter the kingdom of God (John 3:3,5). The popular term, "born again," literally translates "born from above." If we must be born from above before we can see and enter the kingdom of God, then it must be important to know what it means.

The first Adam was fallen. Every person is born of his bloodline and, therefore, is also fallen. "For all have sinned and fall short of the glory of God" (Rom. 3:23). Each of us is a spirit with a soul (personality) which lives in a body. Our bodies are not who we are, but are only the houses in which we live out our earthly existence. Though our bodies decay at death, the real persons that we are live on after death. There are only two places departed human spirits can go: heaven or hell. Unless we are born from above, we cannot see and enter the kingdom of God. We cannot go to heaven.

God, the Father, became man in the person of Jesus Christ. He called Himself the Son of God. He is regarded in scripture as the "last Adam" (1 Cor. 15:45). He lived according to the righteousness of God. He was crucified, died, was buried, arose, ascended into heaven and sent His Holy Spirit back to earth from the day of Pentecost until now to carry out His divine purposes in mankind.

When we, through faith in Jesus Christ, receive Jesus, we receive His Spirit. The very breath of God is blown into our human spirits, and we are quickened to new lives in Christ. We are literally born from above. We are no longer of the bloodline of the first Adam, but have been born into the bloodline of the last Adam, Jesus Christ. At that moment of saving faith, we become spiritual babies in Christ Jesus, and the salvation process begins.

We are born from above when we repent of having not made Jesus Christ lord of our lives. True repentance will come only as the result of God's gracious act of revealing Christ Jesus to us. Salvation is entirely the result of God's grace and has nothing to do with what we deserve or what we can do for ourselves. The apostle Paul says in his letter to the Ephesians, "For by grace are you saved through faith; and that not of yourselves: it is the gift of God: not of works, lest any man should boast" (Eph. 2:8-9).

Yet, we dare not live our lives passively through, hoping someday that something dramatic will happen to us to give us that sense of assurance that we have been born from above. No one knows when death might swallow us up. This decision cannot be made after death. Therefore, before we die, we must make a deliberate decision to repent and make Jesus Christ lord of our lives.

The sinner's prayer

This decision is most adequately made through what is commonly called "the sinner's prayer." There are no easy steps to salvation. It is not a thing we do, like joining a club. For Jesus, the person, is the good news from God, and salvation is the result of a personal and continual relationship with Jesus Christ as Lord. So, praying "the sinner's prayer" does not in itself merit salvation. Yet, when we sincerely pray the sinner's prayer with a broken and contrite heart, the Lord hears and answers. It is our invitation to God in Christ to come into our lives, not only to take up residency but rulership.

Here are the main points in a sinner's prayer that help us to express to God the desire of our repentant hearts. If you have any doubt in your heart that you are a born again son of the living God, you can get that assurance now by sincerely taking the following steps in prayer.

61

Recognize you are a sinner, lost, hell-bound, and in need of salvation.

Confess to God that you are a sinner; admit it to Him. Ask Him to bring to mind all the sins for which you need forgiveness.

Name those sins to Him and ask Him to forgive you for them. Then, ask Him to break the power of sin over your life.

Ask Him to remove your sins from you and deliver you from all unrighteousness.

Confess that Jesus Christ is the Son of the living God.

Invite Jesus Christ to come into your being and live His life through you.

Declare to Him that you want Him to be lord of your whole life.

Ask Him to breathe on you with His Holy Spirit and cause you to be born from above.

Ask Him to fill, immerse, and clothe you with His Holy Spirit that you might have the power to live the Christian life daily.

Ask Him to give you the gifts of the Spirit as He desires and stir them up in you that you might serve others in the power of His Spirit.

Having made a prayer of this, and believing in your heart that you are now born from above by the Holy Spirit of God, tell someone else about your decision to make Jesus Christ the lord of your life.

Follow-up

God, the Father, continues to parent us through the person of His Holy Spirit who instructs us in His word.

The word of God tells us that water baptism is a necessary first act of obedience for every new believer (Acts 2:38). Be baptized immediately and get into fellowship with other believers who will help you grow in the Lord.

At this time of saving faith, you are a baby Christian. You have only begun your new life in Christ. The new birth is not the goal of the Christian life; it is the beginning of it, and you cannot begin any other way. It is easy to get discouraged and tempted back into the world. That is why the scripture exhorts believers to be steadfast and to not forsake the assembling of themselves together for the purpose of encouraging one another (Heb. 10:25).

Study your Bible in order to know the word of God for yourself. Develop the pattern of talking to God continually through prayer. Fellowship with Him at all times in the Holy Spirit.

The born again experience is a real, actual transformation that occurs within you. You literally become a new creature—a new creation. You were created by God to become a son of God in the family of God that you might glorify Him and enjoy Him forever.

Once we are born again we become one with Him—we are in the Father and the Father is in us. We can now be fathered by the Father of fathers who alone puts *the dad* in us so that we can in turn become fathers.

I have found *the dad* in me and He is Almighty God, Jehovah, the great I AM, God Most High, Jesus—He is my heavenly Father. I am still learning more about Him, and He is still cultivating that dad seed within me.

PROCESSING GUIDE

Have you met Father-God through a rebirth experience? If not, did you pray the "sinner's prayer" suggested on page 65?

If so, write a brief statement of your experience.

What do you think and feel about being a son in relationship to God as a Father?

What plans have you made to receive water baptism?

Write your thoughts and feelings about the ideas presented in this chapter.

Chapter 8

BECOMING SONS FIRST

I went to my fortieth high school reunion and visited with one of my schoolmates who had built a very successful car dealership in my hometown.

"What have you been doing with yourself lately?" I asked.

He settled back in his chair as a satisfied smile swept across his face: "Mostly messing with my sixty head of cattle on my farm out in the country," he answered. "My sons are running the business."

God had been teaching me some of what it meant to be a son of God and how we, as His sons, are in business with Him. We are *Father and Sons, Inc.,* as one teacher put it.

When my friend told me his sons were running the business, a flood of analogies rushed through my mind. I do not know the names of his sons, and what follows is strictly fiction. I'll call one of the sons "Junior."

From the time he was just a little boy, Junior liked to hang out with his dad at the dealership. I imagine him sitting in his daddy's oversized chair with his feet propped up on the desk just like Dad. Dad was the greatest. When he was a little older Junior tagged along with Dad to the bank and watched him borrow hundreds of thousands of dollars to pay for a new shipment of cars coming in.

One day he decided that he would go alone to the bank and try to do what he had seen his dad do. "Hi! I'm Junior. Remember me? I want to borrow a zillion dollars for my dad. He's got another load of cars coming in. Just put it in his bank account like you did for him."

The bank officer covered his smile, leaned forward from behind his desk, and carefully explained, "Well, Junior, you seem to be catching on to your dad's business. I'm sure that one of these days you will be carrying on just like your dad. But we have a little problem here. We cannot make that kind of a loan unless your dad is here to do it himself or has told us that you are authorized to do it in his name."

Junior understood...sort of. He shrugged his shoulders and went his way.

Thirty or so years later, Junior walks into that same bank and talks to the bank officer who, without a question, loans him his needed capital. The difference? He worked his way up through the business, proved himself a faithful son, and now has his dad's authorization to do business in his name.

I was convinced, though my friend did not say so, that he had not removed himself from general oversight of the business. His sons may be running the business, but they do not own it. They may have great latitude in certain areas, but they are running it according to their daddy's will and ways. The dealership is still in their dad's name.

Graduated authority

When I was a little boy, spiritually speaking, in my Father-God's house, I had certain but few privileges. Mostly, I was taught and disciplined by God who faithfully looked after all of my needs. As I grew up under submission to my Father-God, I learned of His will and ways. I learned primarily by watching His Son, my big brother, Jesus, and by the discipline of His Holy Spirit.

I learned more and more about how He did business and how He expects His sons to do His business for Him. He gradually turned more authority over to me as I proved obedient and faithful to do His will and walk in His ways. I came to a place one day where I could say certain things and they would have to happen just because I said so.

I cannot say just anything I please, but there are some things I know are right to declare because I know my Father's will and ways. They are the kinds of things He would say, and He has given me authority to say them on His behalf. I know not to be arrogant or presumptuous about these things. I take this responsibility very seriously as I believe my friend's sons do when they go to the bank to borrow great sums of money.

Many of us as new Christians were taught that we had authority in Jesus' name. We declared all sorts of things in His name, but nothing changed. We may have become discouraged, and some may have even fallen away in disbelief. We were not taught that we had to grow up into becoming responsible sons before we could exert authority in certain areas. We were not seasoned enough to appropriately use that authority.

We have to be a son before we can become a father. We do not jump into the world and automatically become dads. We grow into that. As a son we have to learn how to depend upon Father-God for every need we may have. We have to subject ourselves willfully and joyfully to his discipline in our lives. All He wants to do anyway is to raise us up to be fathers in authority, to bear His image, and do business according to His will and His ways.

Sonship

When I use the term sonship, I'm not just talking about being little children—sons and daughters. I'm talking about a kind of maturity we come into when several key elements are present in our lives—things such as submission to authority, obedience, trust, humility, and self-giving love.

A boy cannot come easily, if at all, into sonship if fatherhood is not present to call it forth. Sonship goes with fatherhood. Fatherhood is essentially the presence of *the dad.*

God Himself is the highest and most perfect embodiment of fatherhood. He makes His presence known to us and calls us forth as His spiritual sons. "For the earnest expectation of the creature waits for the manifestation of the sons of God....For whom He foreknew, He also predestined to be conformed to the image of His Son, that He might be the firstborn among many brethren. Moreover whom He did predestine, He also called: and whom He called, He also justified: and whom He justified, He also glorified" (Rom. 8:19, 29-30). What God wants in His spiritual house is the same as what He wants in the natural families of His people—sons conformed into the image of His Son. The person of Jesus Christ defines sonship at its best.

Sons learn submission to authority

God is the highest authority in the universe. He has delegated the dad to be the authority in the lives of his children. The mom has authority, but it is different and far less compelling. A healthy, functional dad who is present in the life of his children will teach authority and submission.

Submission to authority is very important to God. We are to submit ourselves one to another (Eph. 5:21), to pastoral oversight (Heb. 13:17), to God (Jas. 4:7), and to every ordinance of man (1 Pet. 2:13). Wives are to submit to husbands (Eph. 5:22; Col. 3:18), and younger men are to submit to older men (1 Pet. 5:5). If we as children do not learn submission in the home, it becomes difficult to learn how to submit to the righteousness of God (Rom. 10:3).

Jesus was totally submitted to His heavenly Father, therefore He learned authority and had authority. "For he taught them as one having authority, and not as the scribes" (Matt. 7:29).

So, sonship involves submission to authority. The son who learns submission will learn how to be in authority.

The dad is a righteous authority when he himself is under the authority of Jesus.

Sons learn obedience

Obedience is the mark of spiritual sonship. "For as many as are led by the Spirit of God, they are the sons of God" (Rom. 8:14).

Jesus is our example of a son in absolute obedience to his father. He was bound by His love for His father to do only what He saw the Father doing. "Then answered Jesus and said unto them...'The Son can do nothing of Himself, but what He sees the Father do: for whatever He does, the Son does likewise. For the Father loves the Son, and shows Him all things that He Himself does: and He will show Him greater works than these, that you may marvel'" (John 5:19-20). "Then said Jesus unto them, '...I do nothing of myself; but as My Father has taught me, I speak these things'" (John 8:28).

Submission and obedience are closely akin, yet are not the same. One can be obedient without being submissive as is illustrated in the story of the little boy who was told to sit down.

"No. I don't want to sit down."

"I said, 'Sit down!'" the parent sternly mandated.

"No!" he replied.

"If you don't sit down, I will come over there and spank you."

He finally sat down but said, "I may be sitting down on the outside, but I'm still standing up on the inside!"

Obedience is the outward behavior of doing things. Submission reflects an attitude, a condition of the heart. Pure obedience is the fruit of a submissive spirit. Sonship speaks of the kind of sons who are both submissive and obedient. They respond well to fatherhood. They sit down, even on the inside, the first time they are asked.

Paul exhorts, "Children, obey your parents in the Lord: for this is good" (Eph. 6:1) and "Children, obey your parents in all things for this is well pleasing to the Lord" (Col. 3:20).

Obedience and submission does not come naturally to children. These have to be taught and modeled. Children acquire them through discipline (discipleship). Fatherhood disciples sonship; that is, teaches submission and obedience.

Sons learn trust

When true and dependable fatherhood is present, a son learns to put his trust in his father. He may not always understand or even agree with dad's actions, but he goes along with him. The ultimate example of this blind trust occurred between Abraham and his son Isaac.

Abraham was a man under the authority of the Almighty. He was, as it were, a son in obedient submission. Whatever God said, Abraham did. Abraham trusted God as Father. God had made His covenant with Abraham that he would be the father of a multitude.

Abraham, as a son under God, made a father by God, and who acted on blind faith in God, was now asked to sacrifice his son Isaac, the son of promise. Think about that. How could Abraham even think of putting the knife to his son? But have you ever thought about how this looked through Isaac's eyes? Can you imagine the rush of emotions he must have felt when Abraham bound him and laid him upon the altar? There is no indication at all that Isaac put up a struggle.

Isaac could not have surrendered himself to Abraham if he did not trust him. Abraham could not have gone as far as he did had he not trusted in his God.

Isaac asked, "I see the fire and the wood: but where is the lamb for a burnt offering?"

Faith-filled Abraham answered, "God will provide."

Abraham also exercised His trust in God when he earlier told the two men traveling with them, "I and the lad will go over there and worship, and come again to you." He fully expected God would provide, yet he was willing to obey to the end. What trust! At the last moment, an angel commanded Abraham to stay his hand, and God provided another sacrifice—a ram caught in the thicket. (See Gen. 22:1-14 and Heb. 11:17-19.)

Thank God for His provision. God always provides for those who put their trust in Him and obey Him. Such are young men who learn sonship.

Jesus confirmed the role that faith and trust play in our ability to submit to authority. Matthew gives this account: "When Jesus had entered into Capernaum, there came to Him a centurion, beseeching Him and saying, 'Lord, my servant lies at home sick of the palsy, grievously tormented.' And Jesus said to him, 'I will come and heal him.' The centurion answered and said, 'Lord, I am not worthy that you should come under my roof: but speak the word only, and my servant shall be healed. for I am a man under authority, having soldiers under me: and I say to this man, "Go," and he goes; and to another, "Come," and he comes; and to my servant, "Do this," and he does it.' When Jesus heard it, He marveled, and said to them that followed, 'Truly I say to you, I have not found so great faith, no, not in Israel'" (Matt. 8:5-10).

Submission becomes difficult for us when an authority abuses his position and violates us. We lose our trust and confidence in him. If we have been abused by a significant authority figure during our formative years, we may have difficulty ever trusting any authority.

The dad, because he is a man of good character and integrity, builds trust and thereby commands respect for and submission to his authority. He has authority because he is under the authority of Christ.

Sons learn humility

Submission, obedience, and trust work through humility. Humility has to do with being honest and open with ourselves, God, and others. When we are willing to be honest and open with ourselves, we will see the truth about ourselves, and that should always have a humbling effect upon us. Pride hinders our ability to submit to another. Humility frees us to do so.

Sons who learn to humble themselves before older men will find it easier to humble themselves before God. 1 Peter 5:5-6 says, "Likewise, you younger, submit yourselves unto the elder. Yes, all of you be subject one to another, and be clothed with humility: for God resists the proud, and gives grace to the humble. Humble yourselves therefore under the mighty hand of God, that He may exalt you in due time." It is far better for God to lift us up than for us to try to lift ourselves up by the inflated estimations of ourselves.

Sons learn fatherhood

Good fathering is likely to beget good sons. Nevertheless, some sons go bad no matter how good their parenting was. Parents need not wallow in self-blame. How must the father of the prodigal son have felt when his son left home and squandered his inheritance? (See Luke 15:11-24.) Proverbs 22:6 says, "Train up a child in the way he should go: and when he is old, he will not depart from it." The scripture says that the prodigal son came to his senses and returned home. Could the father's training of him as a child have had a bearing on that decision as well?

Good sons become good fathers just as good trees bear good fruit. The father is put into the son so that the son can become a father. And when the son becomes a father, he still retains the heart of the son within him. The father and the son are one within him. If we know sonship, we will know fatherhood. If we know fatherhood, we will know sonship. We cannot separate the two.

We pass through three stages in our spiritual development. We start out as babes and children, then we become sons (young men), and ultimately become fathers. Fathers

71

are children-centered, sons are father-centered, and children are self-centered. God, the Father, is children-centered, and Jesus, the Son, is father-centered. Most of us are self-centered children. We are to mature into sons who are father-centered and onward to fatherhood.

Sonship is a passage to becoming *the dad.* The character attributes a son learns become invaluable attributes of fatherhood.

The character attributes of submission, obedience, trust, and humility teach us how to be in authority. If we do not have these attributes, we will not exercise godly authority. We are not likely to be given authority, and any authority we think we have will be oppressive.

True authority and submission to that authority is liberating. Children who learn to respect boundaries grow up with a comfort and security which brings freedom. Children who are not given boundaries never quite learn who they are and become enslaved to things like fear, insecurity, strife, and greed. A certain amount of structure is freeing; a lack of structure brings anarchy.

Jesus, the pattern Son

If we did not have an earthly model of a dad growing up, we will have to learn how to be a dad from some other source. The perfect source is Father-God who wants to be our dad and cut us loose from our mother's emotional apron strings.

The only way we can learn from God is to first be a son in relationship to God. This means we have to submit to the discipline of the Lord. It means we have to learn obedience just as Hebrews 5:8 said about Jesus: "He learned obedience by the things He suffered."

Jesus, as the Son of God, is the pattern for us to go by in relating to Father-God. He is our only example for learning sonship.

Christian dads are encouraged to be Jesus not only to their own children but to the fatherless children in their communities, especially their community of faith—guiding these boys into becoming sons of God and future dads.

Characteristics of good sons

Jesus loved His Father more than He loved Himself. He proved this by being obedient even unto death (Phil. 2:8). *Agape* (the God-kind of love) has to do with denying self of its willful, self-indulging, and prideful ways. Jesus embarked upon His own trail of self-denial when He overcame the temptations of the devil in the wilderness. He passed through another crisis in the garden of Gethsemane on His way to the cross.

The love that Jesus had for the Father was the driving force behind His compulsion to do His Father's will. He desired nothing else. This drive gave Him His ability to overcome self at every turn.

He began every day in prayer to find out what was on Father's agenda for that day. He only did what He saw His Father doing. He was obedient and faithful to the very end. "Not my will, but Yours."

Isaac had a foretaste of *agape*-love. His love and respect for his father gave him the strength and trust he needed to be willing to lay down his life.

We, as spiritual sons, learn obedience and faithfulness by the things we suffer as well, allowing Christ to crucify our old man of sin nature.

Jesus had to continually submit to the leading of the Holy Spirit in order to know and do the Father's will. Spiritual sons continually submit to the leading of the Holy Spirit.

Jesus had a hunger for righteousness. Spiritual sons have a hunger for righteousness.

He had a passion for holiness. Spiritual sons have a passion for holiness. Holiness is not about "going to church." It is not about "being good." It is not what we do, what we wear, how we fix our hair, or what we say. It has to do with what is going on inside of us as the result of the

Holy Spirit's work within us. It has to do with being conformed as spiritual sons into the image of the pattern Son, Jesus.

Jesus made no provision for the flesh. Spiritual sons of God make no provision for the flesh. We learn to deny our flesh man of its demands, compulsions, and mental obsessions. How do we do that? "Walk in the Spirit, and you shall not fulfill the lusts of the flesh" (Gal. 5:16).

Moving on

We must learn how to be a son before we can know how to be a father. Yet, we cannot put fathering on hold until we all attain to that ideal model of fatherhood. We learn fathering as we learn how to be a son and learn how to be a son as we continue to father. Fathering and sonship go hand in hand. We cannot learn one without the other automatically happening. One cannot exist without the other. There is no such thing as father unless there are children. There is no such thing as children unless there are parents. The terms suggest each other's existence.

Only God, who is the ultimate embodiment of fatherhood, can bring us into true sonship. Let us yield to Him and His Holy Spirit that He may do so.

PROCESSING GUIDE

Briefly describe the most memorable time that you were obedient to do something positive when asked to do so.

Did you have a healthy respect for the authorities who asked this act of obedience of you?

How do you see trust playing a part in this act of obedience?

How do you see humility playing a part in this act of obedience?

How did this or other acts of obedience prepare you for manhood?

Briefly describe the most memorable time that you were disobedient. What, if any, were the consequences?

Briefly describe how your father contributed to cutting you loose from your mother's emotional apron strings.

What characteristics of Jesus as the perfect Son in relationship to His Father-God do you want for yourself? Examples: submission, obedience, trust, humility, and fatherhood.

Pray and ask God to call forth those characteristics within you.

Write your thoughts and feelings about the ideas presented in this chapter.

Chapter 9

THE DAD'S TRUE VOCATION

"**N**ot in the wildest dreams of Buddy and Helen Watts did they ever think that the fifth child born to them of six children, in a rural community in Oklahoma, in a poor black neighborhood, on the east side of the tracks...that their son, Junior, would some day grow up to be called Congressman. But after all—this is America."

With that remark, J. C. Watts concluded his rousing speech at the 1996 Republican Convention. He had already established, however, that "there is one title I cherish a whole lot more than the title Congressman, and that's the title Dad." Being a dad is a man's true vocation.

When we hear the term "vocation," we generally think of the occupation one is particularly suited for or qualified to do. Sometimes we simply use that term to identify one's job, even if the individual is not particularly gifted for it.

However, a "vocation" really has to do with one's calling. Most of us feel "called" to do one thing or another. Some people believe they were called to be preachers, teachers, medical professionals, politicians, business persons, housewives, social workers, counselors, hairdressers, carpenters, electrical engineers, etc.

We who feel called to a particular vocation take our callings seriously. We commit large amounts of money and time preparing ourselves for these careers. It is especially rewarding when we can find employment that supports us to do those things we feel called to do.

There is little doubt that many of us men feel called to do different things that provide important services to others and permit us to make a living in the process. I, nevertheless, believe that these are our *secondary* callings and not our *primary* ones.

Family is *the dad's* true vocation

I believe that our primary vocation, our true calling is to be the husband and father in our families.

The original meaning of the word *husband* is "householder." It has to do with caring for the affairs of the household. It includes the overall stewardship given to *the dad* toward the whole family.

The husband and father is the shepherd of his family. A shepherd is one who herds, guards, and tends sheep. Shepherds who care for and guide a congregation of people are commonly called "pastors." Shepherd and pastor are synonymous terms.

God did not call Abraham to be a businessman, a tentmaker, or a trader; He called him to be the father of a multitude. In the same way, God also calls us to be fathers. Abraham, nevertheless, occupied himself with things that provided for the care and nurture of his family. In the same way, God calls us to occupations that enable us to provide for our families, and these occupations often serve others as well.

However, our *primary* vocation is family. That is our job, our priority, our focus, and our life's goal whether we are conscious of it or not, whether we are pursuing it or avoiding it. Whatever else we do is intended to support this primary vocation. This call of God for a man to be the shepherd of his family rests within his bosom.

Family is *the dad's* function

Because of this calling, *the dad* has a function in the family that no one else can perform. A woman left alone to raise the children has to do the best she can, but she can never be a father to them, nor can the father be a mom to them. The kids need both fathering and mothering. These are two distinctly different roles and functions. Every child has a vacuum in his soul that needs to be filled with a mom and a dad.

When either or both of these are missing, the child experiences some degree of social, emotional, and spiritual deficiency. Such deficiency is abusive even though such absence is unavoidable at times. Parents who are left to raise their children alone are not always to blame. They are to be encouraged and helped by others in their families and communities of faith as much as possible.

May God bless the good men and women who have given abandoned children a home and a life full of love and care. May God bless stepparents who provide an environment of love, appreciation, and respect for one another in those difficult situations. We will have to make the best of what we have. Ultimately, however, we want to work toward the restoration of men to godliness that they may reclaim their calling as husbands and dads, that they may see this calling as their primary vocation and not relinquish it to the moms, grandparents, or stepdads. No one can completely fill the father role as can the genetic dad of the child when he is righteously performing his vocation.

Family is *the dad's* focus

As dads, flames of jealousy should rage in our spirits to fight for our families and our right to righteously father our children. Rather than running from family responsibility, we leap in the midst of it. Rather than balking at the challenge of responsible fathering, we charge head-on toward it. Rather than fading into oblivion, we stare our insecurities and fears in the face and declare, "No more! We will stand up in our calling from God."

We come out of hiding in cyberspace, the locker room at the local Y, our tackle boxes, our pickup trucks—the fog of our obsessions—to focus on those domestic responsibilities that belong to us. We discover that our families are more than something we have to work into our guarded activities now and then. We discover that we belong in the toy box with our children.

We learn how to focus on what God has called us to be by observing how God fathers us. We make it our job to do what we know to do, leaning heavily upon the grace and mercy of a forgiving God. We strive to become as competent in our jobs as dads as we are in our secondary vocations.

God wants us to have the best job possible as a provision for our families. He wants us to do our best on that job. But He wants that in order for us to fulfill our primary role as husbands and dads. Family is our main focus.

Family is *the dad's* possession

Certainly family belongs to all of its members. Mom has made the greatest sacrifice of all bringing forth the children. She is going to feel quite naturally and rightfully possessive of her family. We do not want to take that away. Yet, dad needs to see his unique ownership role of his family if he is to take on his responsibility and stewardship of them.

In the spirit of Abraham, the dad's family came out of his loins and is an extension of the man himself. His family is his own possession just as we, as God's family, belong to God.

God, as Father, wanted a people for His own possession when He chose Israel. Deuteronomy 7:6 explains, "For you are a holy people unto the Lord your God: the Lord your God has chosen you to be a special people unto Himself, above all people who are upon the face of the earth."

Father-God reaffirmed this calling in the New Testament toward His assembly of called-out-ones. We read in 1 Peter 2:9, "But you are a chosen generation, a royal priesthood, a holy nation, a peculiar people; that you should show forth the praises of Him who has called you out of darkness into His marvelous light."

79

Though family is the dad's possession, this ownership does not license us dads to be dictators. We are not autocrats and our family members are not our slaves. On the contrary, we exist to serve them and to meet their needs.

Family is *the dad's* responsibility

If family is the dad's calling and possession, then family is his responsibility.

God has placed the husband as the head of the wife which automatically makes him the head or shepherd of his family. He is responsible for them. He has the call and the anointing from God to be the head. He cannot abdicate or relegate that responsibility to another.

Many of us men enjoy the authority that goes with being the head of the family, but we do not take too well to the responsibility that goes with the authority. All authority carries with it corresponding responsibilities. Authority is a responsibility in and of itself. Whenever we are given responsibility, we become the authority in that area of administration. We cannot have one without the other.

The dad is responsible to God for what happens to his family. A woman may end up having to take responsibilities that she is not supposed to have, but she will not be held responsible for what was not hers.

Family is *the dad's* stewardship

A steward by definition is one who manages another person's property, finances, or other affairs. In other uses of the term, a steward may be one who is in charge of the household affairs of a large estate and whose duties may include supervision of the kitchen and servants, management of household accounts, or one who acts as a supervisor or administrator for another (as in finances or property).

The dad's family is his true vocation, function, focus, possession, and responsibility but only because it has been given to him by God for his stewardship. For in reality God is the sole possessor of us all, including the family. The very idea of family belongs to Him.

We, as husbands and fathers, have been given stewardship on behalf of God for certain areas of administration by virtue of our calling as men. Our stewardship extends to the full limit of our areas of administration.

We are stewards over all life areas pertaining to ourselves and our family members. These major life areas are spiritual, physical, emotional, relational, sexual, mental, financial, educational, social, political, careers and jobs, and recreational. We are responsible for what our children read, see, listen to, and learn about God. We are responsible for their health, well-being—everything.

The dad who has the Spirit of God within him will begin to sense his stewardship responsibilities in all of these areas of his life.

Moreover, he has various stewardship responsibilities toward his family members whether they are his wife and children, brothers and sisters, aging parents, or to some extent, his extended natural family. If the adult men in the home today were acting responsibly as stewards in all of these life areas, there would be less homelessness and little need for public welfare.

Once we dads see that family is our true vocation, we will see that being *the dad* is also a high honor and privilege that God has bestowed upon us.

PROCESSING GUIDE

Did your father make family his primary vocation?

If not, how might your home life have been different if he had made family his primary vocation?

If married, do you make your family your primary vocation?

If not, what might you change to make your family

81

your primary vocation?

How willing are you to do this?

Write a specific statement of responsibility about each life area you can think of that is in your care; such as spiritual, physical, emotional, relational, sexual, mental, financial, educational, social, political, professional (careers and jobs), and recreational responsibilities.

What goals do you have or need to have for meeting your responsibilities in those areas?

What progress are you making in achieving those goals?

Write your thoughts and feelings about the ideas presented in this chapter.

Chapter 10

ELDER
CHARACTERISTICS
IN THE MAKING

We come into the family of God as little children. Little children are completely dependent upon their parents. This is the way God wants us to be toward Him. He wants us to have unrestrained dependence upon Him, but He does not want us to remain as little children because children are typically self-centered.

God wants us to grow up to become sons of obedience. Sons of obedience turn their concerns away from self to seek the will of their father.

Ultimately, God wants us to mature and become fathers in His Kingdom. The father's primary concern is for the children. True elders in the Kingdom of God are spiritual fathers.

Elders in the Kingdom

The term elder comes from the Greek word *presbuteros* which literally means "an older man." This likely refers to the chronological age of the men in an assembly of called-out-ones. It most certainly has to do with spiritual maturity that can only come with the passing of years in the faith.

The apostle Paul wrote Timothy (whom he called his "own son in the faith") and listed certain qualifications for an elder:

"A bishop [literally, "overseer"][14] then must be blameless, the husband of one wife, vigilant, sober, of good behavior, given to hospitality, able to teach; not given to wine, no striker, not greedy of filthy lucre; but patient, not a brawler, not covetous; one who rules well his own house, having children in subjection with all gravity; (for if a man does not know how to rule his own house, how shall he take care of the church [assembly] of God?) not a novice, lest being lifted up with pride he falls into the condemnation of the devil. Moreover he must have a good report of those who are on the outside; lest he fall into reproach and the snare of the devil" (1 Tim. 3:2-7).

These qualifications have to do with character and integrity. True elders in the Kingdom of God are spiritual fathers called of God to feed and oversee the family of God. They are to be father figures for all of the natural fathers of families.

Elders in the home

While not every one of us is called of God to be an elder in the Kingdom of God, these qualifications for elders stand as a model for all men who desire godly character. They serve as guideposts for those of us who would learn how to be overseers and shepherds in our own homes. We should aspire to be men of such character and integrity. We want the Holy Spirit to cultivate these characteristics in each of us.

But what do these look like when they are in operation? Let us take each one of these characteristics and see how they might apply to husbands and dads.

---

[14]Elder, bishop, and pastor are synonymous terms in the New Testament. This is most clearly seen in Acts 20:17,28: Paul called for the elders of Ephesus to join him in Miletus. Among other things he said, "Take heed therefore unto yourselves, and to all the flock over the which the Holy Ghost has made you *overseers* [bishops], to *feed* [shepherd, pastor] the church of God."

Without reproach[15]

"A bishop then must be above reproach." The Greek word for "above reproach" is *anepilemptos*. It has to do with being above criticism, shame, and disgrace. In the King James Version, this word is translated "blameless" and in the New International Version (NIV), "above reproach." *An Expository Dictionary of New Testament Words* by W. E. Vine says it literally means "'that cannot be laid hold of,' hence, 'not open to censure, irreproachable.'"[16]

Character has to do with who we are—being, not doing; character and not character-acting. It cannot be faked. Nevertheless, we are still in the process of becoming who we are in Christ. Until we come to that place of perfection, we want to *do* our best to *be* blameless. We want to live our lives in such a way that no one can find legitimate fault with us.

Husband of one wife

Most scholars agree that the phrase "husband of one wife" refers to the practice of polygamy which was in widespread practice among the Gentiles of that time. Others believe this should include divorcés as well. This scripture does not say explicitly whether this includes divorcés, but we are safe to assume that it does speak against polygamy. Polygamous marriages have no ground for acceptance according to New Testament teachings.

The New Testament husband takes his cue from the elders in the assembly and commits to being a one-woman

---

[15]This and the following characteristics have been taken from *The Interlinear Greek-English New Testament* which uses The Nestle Greek Text with a Literal English Translation by The Reverend Alfred Marshall D. Litt, © Samuel Bagster and Sons Ltd. 1958, as found in *The Zondervan Parallel New Testament in Greek and English* (Grand Rapids, MI: Zondervan, 1977).

[16]W. E. Vine, Jr., *Vine's Complete Expository Dictionary of Old and New Testament Words*, eds. Merrill F. Unger and William White (Nashville: Thomas Nelson Publishers, 1985), 68.

man. He is not a flirtatious, womanizing, adulterous, pornography-using, sexually addicted man. There are few things, if any, more damaging to family than adultery.

The dad is faithful and devoted to his wife and children, and the whole assembly knows this about him.

Temperate

The Greek word for "temperate" is *nephalios* which comes from a root word having to do with being free from the influence of intoxicants. It speaks to being clear-headed and self-controlled. It has been used in association with "watchfulness" but is not the word for "watchfulness."[17] The King James Version translated it "vigilant" and "sober."

The dad is both sober and sober-minded.

Sensible

The Greek word for "sensible" is *sophron* which is in accordance with having good sense and showing self-control. The King James Version translates it "good behavior" and the NIV, "respectable." It has also been rendered "prudent" and "sober-minded." Sober-minded in this context has to do with how we think as well as what we think about.

The dad is given to wisdom, knowledge, and understanding. He applies practical and reasonable consideration to his decisions. He is not impulsive in his thinking or actions. He seeks the counsel of others. He does not rationalize bad behavior. Rather, he behaves in such a way as to gain the respect of those in his universe of relationships, especially those of his own household.

Orderly

The Greek word for "orderly" is *kosmios* which has to do with being decent, modest, and orderly in appearance

---

[17]Ibid., 583.

and behavior. The King James Version translates it "good behavior" and the NIV, "respectable."

The dad has order in his life. If our personal lives are disorderly, our whole household will feel the effects. We want to progress toward the goal of being respectable, decent, modest, and orderly in all aspects of our lives.

Given to hospitality

The Greek word for "hospitality" is *philoxenos* which is a combination of two Greek words: *philos* which has to do with affectionate, brotherly love and *xenos* which denotes a stranger. Thus, it could be translated, "receiving a stranger with brotherly affection." The King James Version translates this word "entertain strangers" in Hebrews 13:2.

Sadly, many dads have allowed their own family members to become strangers as well as becoming a stranger to them. *The dad* is "given to hospitality" first of all to the members of his own household. He receives them affectionately.

Able to teach

The Greek word for "apt (able) to teach" is *didaktikos* which has to do with giving instruction.

The dad accepts responsibility not only to teach his children in the scope of his knowledge and ability, but also sees to it that his children learn what they need to know beyond his scope of knowledge and ability. We and our wives are team players in the education of our children.

All of these other character traits of *the dad* as shown here further qualify us to teach our children. We communicate much to our children by being men of character and integrity. Men who teach have a special influence on the children they teach.

Not excessive drinker

The Greek word for "excessive drinker" is *paroinos* which literally means "at wine," or "tarrying at wine." It has been translated "drunkard" and "given to strong wine." The King James Version translates it "not given to wine" which would suggest total abstinence and the NIV, "not given to much wine" which suggests temperance. Vine's dictionary says that it has more to do with the effects of drinking wine than it does with the actual act of drinking wine—thus, a brawler.[18]

This certainly addresses those individuals who cannot hold their liquor, who cannot maintain sobriety and proper behavior.

Many people "given to" the drink are victims of alcoholism. The drink has taken control. Total abstinence is a must for alcoholics. Abstinence is not a bad rule for all of us since none of us can be sure we will be free from alcoholism. Sometimes we cannot know until after a few years of slowly getting in deeper and deeper.

It is difficult for an alcoholic to believe he is really an alcoholic. Denial is another name for the disease. The man who is given to the influence of intoxicants will be a troubled man. He is most likely the addict in his dysfunctional, shame-based family. So, if we even *think* we may be alcoholics, we need to admit it and get help. Much loving support is available today.

The dad will seek freedom from such bondage for his own sake as well as that of his family's.

Not a striker, but forbearing

The Greek word "striker" is *plekte* and has to do with hitting others. It may be associated with brawling. The King James Version translates it "no striker" and separates it from the word "patient" (forbearing). The NIV keeps these two words in juxtaposition just as the Greek

---

[18]Ibid., 77.

has it and translates it "not violent, but gentle."

Strikers are full of rage due possibly to unresolved issues in their lives. They are physically abusive control addicts. They try to control others with violence or threats of violence. Their victims are usually the members of their own household—the battered wife and child.

Strikers can be verbally abusive as well, causing emotional trauma to the members of their household.

Spiritual strikers try to control the behavior of others with religious legalism. They require perfection, and their acceptance of others is based upon performance.

Strikers operate under a double standard whether they are physically, verbally, or spiritually abusive. It is OK to make mistakes themselves, but it is not OK for others to make mistakes. They are unforgiving of the shortcomings of others. Their own insecurities are so great that they find it too painful to admit their own shortcomings, so they remain in denial about themselves, their problems, and their shortcomings.

The dad is not a striker. He is not violent, but is gentle. His voice, his touch, and his personality are gentle. That gentleness is like a security blanket for all. His wife and children know that they can depend on dad to hear them out and comfort them with his soft and gentle words. He explains his reasons, thereby imparting understanding and wisdom.

This is not to say a man can never get angry or raise his voice, but a man is to control his spirit rather than having his emotions control him. "He who is slow to anger is better than the mighty; and he who rules his spirit than he who takes a city" (Prov. 16:32). "He who has no rule over his own spirit is like a city that is broken down, and without walls" (Prov. 25:28).

Forbearing

The Greek word for "forbearing" is *epieikes* which means gentle, forbearing, considerate. The King James

Version translates it "patient" and the NIV, "gentle." Philippians 4:5, using this word, exhorts us all: "Let your moderation [gentleness, graciousness, forbearance, reasonableness] be known unto all men."

Uncontentious

The Greek word used for "uncontentious" is *amachos* which literally has to do with "not fighting." The King James Version translates it "not a brawler" and the NIV, "not quarrelsome."

The dad is a peacemaker who lives out such principles of Christ as "love your enemies," "turn your other cheek," and "do good to those who despitefully use you." Jesus taught, "Blessed are the peacemakers: for they shall be called the children of God" (Matt. 5:9).

Not avaricious

The Greek word for "not avaricious" is *aphilarguros* which has to do with not being covetous. The King James Version translates it "not greedy of filthy lucre" and the NIV, "not a lover of money."

Any man who is obsessed with material gain is a likely candidate for the pursuit of it in an illegal, unethical, or immoral manner. Eventually he will do anything to get it. He is never satisfied with what he has but is addicted to "more." He will be attempting gain for self and not in consideration of spiritual and godly causes.

Moreover, the man of greed is very likely to become an absentee husband and dad. His riches may buy him power and prominence in the world, but he may be a disaster to the family in the home. Anyone who gets in his way will be hurt. He will use people for his own advancement.

There is nothing wrong with having wealth or wanting the very best for our families. The apostle John wrote, "Beloved, I wish above all things that you may prosper and be in health, even as your soul prospers" (3 John 1:2). Wealth in and of itself is neutral, neither good nor evil. A man crosses the line, however, when he becomes obsessed with his desire for riches. Wealth becomes his god, his object of worship. As with any idol god, it ends up controlling him. He will soon adopt the philosophy of the thief, "What is yours is mine, I'll take it."

The dad does not covet more for the sake of having more. He does not covet his neighbor's wife or property but learns to be content in whatever state he finds himself. This peace and contentment transfers over to his family members.

Rules his own household well, having children in subjection with all gravity

The Greek word for "rule" is *proistemi* which has to do with being a leader, having authority over, managing, caring for, giving help. The King James Version reads "rules well his own house" and the NIV, "he must manage his own family well." Vine says this word for "rule" literally means "'to stand before,' hence, 'to lead, attend to' (indicating care and diligence)."[19]

The dad is a man who is in possession of his own soul, has a quiet confidence about himself, has gained the respect of his family, and can be trusted as the leader in his house. His children are in subjection to him in all gravity. Vine says that "gravity" in this sense "denotes 'venerableness, dignity'; it is a necessary characteristic of the life and conduct of Christians."[20]

Ruling the household does not mean being a dictator. Subjection is not oppression. Subjection is a voluntary act in response to love, trust, and respect. Respect is earned, not demanded.

The dad is a caring, supportive, understanding, fun-loving man who knows when and how to properly discipline his children and, thereby, earns their respect. They will learn the meaning of respect in the process.

---

[19]Ibid., 540.
[20]Ibid., 278.

Not a neophyte

The Greek word for "neophyte" is *neophutos*. It is a combination of *neos* which means "new" and *phuo* which means "to bring forth, produce" according to Vine.[21] In the context of the verse it means, "not a new convert." The King James Version translates the phrase "not a novice" and the NIV, "He must not be a recent convert."

Paul explains that a novice should not be made an elder "lest being lifted up with pride he falls into the condemnation of the devil."

All dads are going to be novices at first. The major problem with young men becoming dads today is the lack of modeling that has gone before them. This most important aspect of a man's life receives the least amount of training and attention.

It is never too late for us to improve upon our skills as husbands and dads. We can learn from each other.

To have a good witness

The Greek word for "witness" is *marturia* which has to do with testimony, being a witness, having opportunity to testify. The King James Version translates it "good report" and the NIV, "good reputation."

The character and integrity associated with *the dad* is a witness to those who are on the outside of the community of faith. Being a good witness goes beyond being blameless. It suggests that we are to live our lives in such a manner that others will be able to see Jesus in us. By all means, the members of our own household need to see Jesus. The husband is a type of Christ in the home. If he truly has the nature of Jesus in him, that will be seen everywhere he goes. He will *be* a walking witness.

"Neither do men light a candle and put it under a bushel, but on a candlestick; and it gives light to all who are in the house" (Matt. 5:15).

---

[21]Ibid., 436.

As we dads begin to take on these elder characteristics, we will teach our children by example. It is generational. Dads get *the dad* so we can pass it on to our sons who grow up to pass it on to their sons.

PROCESSING GUIDE

Write about a recent occasion when your character or integrity was tested and ask yourself: on a scale of one to ten, with ten signifying perfection in your performance, how did you measure up to being above reproach, temperate, sensible, orderly, hospitable, forbearing (patient), uncontentious, generous, helpful, and a good witness?

What could you have done differently to up your grade in any of these areas?

Apply that test frequently to challenging situations in your life. Such a practice should help sensitize you to respond differently in the future.

Write your thoughts and feelings about the ideas presented in this chapter.

Chapter 11

A MAN IN SERVANTHOOD

Greatness in the family of God is not determined by popular vote. It is not a matter of who has the most power, prestige, money, or the highest position and praise. It is awarded to the meek and humble who serve without regard to these things.

Jesus explained to His disciples, "If any man desire to be first, the same shall be last of all, and servant of all" (Mark 9:35). On another occasion he said, "He who is greatest among you shall be your servant" (Matt. 23:11).

Scripture speaks of Jesus as a servant: "Behold My Servant, whom I have chosen..." (Matt. 12:18). There are many references in which the apostles spoke of themselves as servants. Galatians 5:13 exhorts, "Brethren...by love serve one another." Given these examples, it is clear that *the dad* is to be a servant to his family.

Servanthood

I regularly attended a Christian men's luncheon that met in a very nice restaurant. We would all gather, visit with each other, eat our bountiful meal, share our testimonies, pray for one another, and go home. I always had a good time.

One day I noticed our waiter standing against the wall with his arms folded, unassuming and waiting for the next man to come in and take his seat. He quietly went over to him and asked, "Coffee or tea?" He did this to each one of

94

us. Each of us answered but hardly noticed him. After he finished serving one individual, he would resume his posture against the wall, waiting for the next man to come in. This was characteristic of the near invisible manner in which he served us throughout our meal.

On this particular day, I felt as though the Holy Spirit nudged me and told me to look around at all of these Christian men in the room. "Listen to them," He said. Some were, admittedly, rather loud, arrogant, and boastful about what God had done in their lives. Then He told me to look at the waiter standing against the wall. As I did, He asked me, "Who is the greatest among you?" The answer was made obvious by the question—it was the waiter. I have never been able to shake that picture of a servant-minister. I really do not want to. It keeps me sober-minded.

Jesus had finished eating His last supper with the twelve when He knelt down to wash their feet. Peter protested, "You shall never wash my feet" (John 13:4-8). Peter thought that it was he who should be washing Jesus' feet. He had not yet understood the irony of true greatness in the Kingdom of God. For in the Kingdom, you see, the greater washes the feet of the lesser.

Dads are thought of as the greatest in the eyes of their kids. But we come into true greatness as God sees it when we become minister-servants in our households—washing, as it were, the feet of our family members.

John the Baptist said, "He [Jesus] must increase, but I must decrease" (John 3:30). So it is with us dads—we must decrease in self-importance so that the Servant-Christ might increase within us. If we serve our families in the way Christ serves His, we will then relate to our families as though they were our disciples. We will see that it is our job, among other things, to bring them to Jesus.

Dad serves his family as the pastor (shepherd), provider, protector, physician, prophet, and priest of his household. He serves in partnership with his wife. She is his helpmate; that is, she helps him serve in these ways.

95

The dad as pastor

Pastors are shepherds. We learn from Ezekiel 34 that the shepherds of Israel were to lead, feed, tend, and heal the sheep. The characteristics of spiritual shepherds (elders), as I have said, set the example for every dad who is the shepherd of his family.

The dad's wife and children are his sheep, at least until that day comes when his daughters marry and his sons take wives for themselves and leave home. The son leaves the covering of his parentage to become the covering for his own wife and family. *The dad* has been put into him so he can go out from his father's house to be *the dad* in his own house.

The daughters leave their father's covering when they marry. Traditionally it has been the father who escorts his daughter to the altar and is asked, "Who gives this woman to be married to this man?" He answers, "I do." In that significant moment in time, dad, who will always be dad, relinquishes his headship and shepherding to that other man in her life. It is not an easy thing for a conscientious dad to do.

The wedding rehearsal was under way. Brenda's dad, Gerald, was practicing his part. "Who gives this woman to be married to this man?" Like a burst of sun through the morning fog, he suddenly realized he could not say, "I do"—he could not give his daughter to this irresponsible man even though his daughter was pregnant by him. So, he pulled the plug on the wedding. Brenda submitted and a bad marriage was prevented. Many daughters today would not have honored their fathers in such a way. Yet, Gerald honored his daughter by acting according to his conscience as the shepherd of his family.

The dad as provider

Men are intuitively "breadwinners." They generally want to work and provide for their families. When their instincts to provide are frustrated by any means, such as physical disability or the inability to find a job, they feel a loss of manhood.

Yet, the man who loses his life in his work abandons his family. The story has been relived over and over in real life and in fiction—the angry adult child lashes out at dad for not having been there for him or her while growing up. Dad answers in dismay, "But I did it for you."

"That is not what I needed, Dad. I didn't need a big house and expensive clothes. I needed you. I needed a hug. I needed a dad."

The dad provides for his family members in all of life's areas over which he has been given jurisdiction. He provides physically, spiritually, mentally, financially, emotionally, and socially.

The dad as protector

In like manner, men are instinctively protectors. As the shepherd and head of his house, he not only has the responsibility for protecting his family, but he has the spiritual authority and weapons to do so. As in all other aspects of ministry to his family, he protects in all the areas of life.

Physically, he protects the health and welfare of the family and maintains a nurturing environment for each of the family members. He protects them from physical harm as much as possible. He teaches them how to avoid danger when it come to strangers, sex, drugs, and other snares of life.

Spiritually, he protects his household by making sure that it has a Holy Spirit environment rather than a demonic one. He teaches his children spiritual, moral, and family values. He disciplines his children righteously. He raises them in the nurture and admonition of the Lord. He is a living epistle in their lives.

He sets the example as a Kingdom-seeking, Bible-reading prayer warrior. As he comes to know for himself the truth of who God is, he becomes better equipped to protect his family from the lies and deceits of false religions, cults, and the doctrines of demons.

He lays a spiritual foundation in the lives of his family upon which his children can build for the rest of their lives. They learn to discern spiritual truths, right from wrong, good from evil, and truth from falsehood.

Relationally, he protects the integrity of the family by being there himself and holding the family together. This job wrongfully falls to other members of the family when the dad is not there, thus creating a dysfunctional, non-nurturing family situation.

Sexually, he protects his family from the invasion of immorality that is so easily accessed today through TV, cyberspace, movies, music, and the print media. He protects them from the potential abuses of others, and from societal permissiveness.

He protects with education, communication, and by example. He keeps an open line with an understanding mind. He protects by filling the cups of his family members with love so that they will not need to go looking for it in all of the wrong places.

The dad as physician

Our role as physicians may not be as clear to most of us men as our other responsibilities, but we are instinctively healers. We want broken things to be fixed, and we usually want to fix them ourselves. We are not medical experts, nor are we expected to be. But as spiritual heads of our households, God has given us the responsibility to provide physical, spiritual, and emotional healing when injuries occur.

The dad heals through prayer. We learn from the scriptures that all believers are given the authority to heal. Mark 16:17-18 reads, "And these signs shall follow them who believe...they shall lay hands on the sick and they shall recover." James 5:14-15 instructs us, "Is any sick among you: Let him call for the elders of the church [assembly of called-out-ones]; and let them pray over him, anointing him with oil in the name of the Lord: and the prayer of faith shall save [heal] the sick, and the Lord shall raise him up..."

Whether it is healing for physical injuries or for broken hearts and dreams, prayer can be a healing tool in dad's hand. We should use it.

The dad heals through love. True godly love is *agape*. *Agape* is the willingness to lay down one's own self-centered interests for the sake and well-being of another. When others are available to us in *agape*, we will know it. We will feel connected and not alone. Love edifies.

The love of Jesus is the ultimate healing for man—spirit, soul, and body. He continues to pour His love into us to give us a reservoir of love to pour into others, beginning with our own families.

The dad heals through caring. It is difficult to separate caring from prayer and *agape*. Prayer is hard work for most of us. I have to lay down my life to pray for others. I have more self-centered things to do with my time. Haven't you? But when I care enough to pray or be there for another person in their neediness, I am showing *agape*. It really helps to know there is at least one person in this world who cares about us, who will check up on us and share his or her life with us. Dads who take the time to listen, play, and work with their children give those children the confidence that their dad really cares for them.

The dad heals through forgiveness. Unforgiveness can be one of the meanest and most destructive spirits in a person. When unforgiveness is left unchecked, it can grow into "a root of bitterness." This unforgiveness and bitterness can lead to emotional and physical problems in the unforgiving one. Unforgiving spirits can be passed down from one generation to another. Yet, in the moment one truly forgives and lets go, healing and peace roll in like a river. *The dad* forgives and sets the example of forgiveness.

The dad heals through understanding and listening ears. So many times in mentoring relationships, all we need is for someone else to just listen. The listener does not need to have the answers or fix our problems. Sometimes we simply need to hear what we have to say by saying it to someone else. Sometimes we just need to get it all out. All of us need to have someone who cares enough to listen with non-critical, non-defensive ears. We dads want to cultivate the habit of hearing others out before we answer. We want to keep the lines of communication open with our wives and children.

The dad heals through soft words. "Sticks and stones may break my bones, but words can never hurt me." Wrong! The Bible charges, "Fathers, do not provoke your children to anger, lest they be discouraged" (Col. 3:21). Critical, debasing, and hurtful words can deeply injure the soul of a child.

If we are tense, full of rage, and perverse in our words toward our children, they will become tense, full of rage, and perverse. Angry and condemning words will provoke the very behavior we are trying to prevent.

On the other hand, if we speak peacefully to our children, they will become peaceful. Edifying words preserve the souls of our children and can even bring healing to the body. Proverbs instructs us well. "A soft answer turns away wrath: but grievous words stir up anger" (Prov. 15:1). "The tongue of the wise will promote health" (Prov. 12:18).

The dad heals through a tender touch. So many children know only abuse from the hands of their caregivers. I have heard many adults say they cannot remember their dads hugging them or touching them in love. We all need to touch and be touched and hugged in a godly manner.

Righteous touching can validate and verify a little person who is suffering from fear and insecurity. It can communicate such messages as, "I love you for who you are and not for how you perform." "It's OK for you to love me." "Everything is going to be OK." "You are safe and secure here." "You are one of us. We are connected and nothing can ever break that."

The dad as prophet

Prophets speak for God. They stand between God and the people to speak to the people on behalf of God. They are supposed to have the word of the Lord. They are seers. They perceive God's heart. They call the people to repentance when they see the people in sin and unrighteousness.

Dads are prophets in the home in the sense that they are to keep the family on course with God. When the family as a unit or any individual member thereof is missing the mark, it is dad's place to call them to repentance. This is done not by speaking harsh words of legalism to them, but by caring, loving, mercy-filled words and wisdom that will woo the wayward back to God.

If the dad is to speak for God, he will need to know the word of God for himself and spend time with God in prayer, seeking wisdom and direction.

The dad as priest

Priests speak for the people. Priests stand between the people and God to speak to God on behalf of the people. In the New Testament, all believers are priests in that we can individually come boldly to the throne of grace.

Nevertheless, *the dad* specifically serves as a priest to his family in several ways.

The priestly function is to hear confessed sins. This takes us back to the physician aspect of *the dad* who takes the time to listen with understanding ears. He is patient, gentle, kind, non-threatening, non-judgmental, and supportive enough to gain his family's confidence in him as a priest. He will be able to mentor his family members to the extent of his willingness to hear their confessions in love and understanding.

The priestly function is to forgive and absolve sin. If we have understanding, we will be able to lead our families to repentance and forgiveness. Jesus has given all believers the authority to forgive and absolve the sins of others. He told his disciples, "Whosoever sins you remit, they are remitted unto them; and whosoever sins you retain, they are retained" (John 20:23). "Remit sins" means to grant forgiveness for a fault, offense, or injury; to forgive, excuse, or pardon. "Retain" means to have and maintain in one's possession; to keep, hold back, reserve.

This priestly function is one that all believers can engage in, and it is especially powerful for dads to function this way. We do not retain the sins of another out of spite or for any unrighteous motivation. *The dad* shows and expresses the forgiving heart of Father-God.

A godly father will discipline his children according to the word of God. As a prophet, he will call them to repentance and as a priest he will absolve them of their sins—all in the name of Jesus. What a release to have someone in authority in our lives to declare, "Your sins are forgiven"!

We all need to see more forgiveness expressed in our relationships, especially within the family. Dads set this example.

The priestly function is to intercede in prayer. To have a person in authority pray over us and intercede for us is a powerful thing. "Confess your faults one to another, and pray one for another, that you may be healed. The effectual fervent prayer of a righteous man avails much" (Jas. 5:16). God hears and answers prayer. He doesn't always give us what we ask for, but when we are in touch with heaven, we will know how to pray according to His will, that His will be done on earth as it is in heaven. We want to depend more upon God in prayer and less upon our own strength.

The priestly function is to speak the blessings. God is moved to action when *the dad* speaks the blessing over his family. We want to discipline ourselves to lay our hands upon our family members at appropriate times and pronounce blessings upon them. We will thereby break the curses, many of which may have been passed down for generations because of the sins and curses of the fathers.

The priestly function is to break the bread and pour the wine of communion. The bread and the wine celebrate the life, crucifixion, resurrection, and ascension of our Lord and Savior, Jesus Christ. *The dad,* in performing these various aspects of service (as pastor, provider, protector, physician, prophet, and priest), demonstrates the life of Jesus. He is breaking the bread of life and pouring out the wine of other-centeredness for his family as the priest of his family. He bonds his family together in a threefold cord that is not quickly broken.

Ask God to give you revelation knowledge of your calling as a servant to your family. Moreover, ask Him to enable you to serve them as Christ serves us all.

PROCESSING GUIDE

Who in your past was an outstanding model of a servant?

How did that person impact your life?

What qualities of servanthood do you recognize in yourself?

What qualities of servanthood do you think you lack?

Write about a recent situation in your life in which the servant qualities of pastor, provider, protector, physician, prophet, or priest came into play? State how you might have handled the situation better with regard to any of these functions.

Write your thoughts and feelings about the ideas presented in this chapter.

Chapter 12

A MAN IN OBEDIENCE

"**B**y faith Abraham, when he was called to go out into a place which he should after receive for an inheritance, obeyed; and he went out, not knowing where he was going" (Heb. 11:8).

We men are called to be something we have never been, to receive an inheritance we have never had. We, like Abraham, are compelled of God to obey Him by faith: to gather up our families and venture into this strange land of spiritual promise—looking for that city which has foundations, whose builder and maker is God.

We are not alone. God is with us, releasing His power upon that which He is calling forth within us. And there are others—multitudes of men who hunger to have *the dad* power released within them. Our individual trails converge on a single path called obedience.

Jesus, preaching to the multitudes, explained the importance of obedience, saying, "Not every one who says to Me, 'Lord, Lord,' shall enter into the kingdom of heaven; but he who does the will of My Father who is in heaven. Many will say to Me in that day, 'Lord, Lord, have we not prophesied in Your name? and in Your name have cast out devils? and in Your name done many wonderful works?' And then will I profess unto them, 'I never knew you: depart from Me, you who work iniquity'" (Matt. 7:21-23).

He illustrated: "Therefore whoever hears these sayings of Mine, and does them, I will compare him to a wise man, who built his house upon a rock: and the rain descended, and the floods came, and the winds blew, and beat upon that house; and it did not fall: for it was founded upon a rock. And every one who hears these sayings of Mine, and does not do them, shall be likened to a foolish man, who built his house upon the sand: And the rain descended, and the floods came, and the winds blew, and beat upon that house; and it fell: and great was the fall of it" (Matt. 7:24-27).

The message here is simple. If we build anything for God according to His blueprint—including family—it will withstand the storms of life that are destined to beat against it; otherwise, it will fall. *The dad* builds his house upon the rock of obedience to God.

God wants an obedient people

God initially chose Israel to be His family and He wanted them to be an obedient people. He spoke to Moses and said, "I have set before you this day a blessing and a curse; a blessing, if you obey the commandments of the Lord your God, which I command you this day: and a curse, if you will not obey the commandments of the Lord your God, but turn aside out of the way which I command you this day, to go after other gods, which you have not known" (Deut. 11:26).

Jesus made it clear that God's family is an obedient people. Someone came to Jesus one day and told Him that His mother and brothers desired to speak to Him. Jesus answered, "Who is My mother? And who are My brothers?" Then, He looked around at the disciples and stretched forth His hand toward them, and said, "See, My mother and My brothers! For whoever shall do the will of My Father who is in heaven, the same is My brother, and sister, and mother" (Matt. 12:46-50).

God wants obedient dads

Men of obedience are under the authority of God who has made them the heads of their households. As long as

105

they remain under God's authority, God spreads His covering over that family. While children may be living in rebellion and are personally accountable to God for their actions, they cannot influence the power and blessing of family as long as the dad remains in obedience to God.

The national life of ancient Israel illustrates this principle. God regarded Israel and Judah as righteous nations as long as their kings acted righteously. Idolatrous kings brought poverty and God's displeasure upon their nation regardless of how righteous some of the people were. Conversely, righteous kings, who honored God and returned to the prescribed worship of the Lord, brought prosperity and God's favor upon their nation regardless of how evil some of the people were.

The well-being of nations throughout history have more to do with the obedience of the heads of state than with the citizens of the state. As the political heads of nations usually go, so go those nations.

Likewise, God honors the family whose dad honors and obeys God, who leads his family as God intended.

Obedience out of love

We obey God because we love Him. Jesus said, "If you love Me, keep My commandments" (John 14:15).

The more we come to know God in Christ, the more we will come to love Him. We have to know God for ourselves. Knowing God has to do with being in a personal relationship with Him; loving Him heart, soul, mind, and strength; loving Him enough to present even our bodies to Him as a living sacrifice (Rom. 12:1).

The more we come to love Him, the more we will be able to trust and obey Him. That grand old hymn still rings true: "Trust and obey, for there's no other way to be happy in Jesus, but to trust and obey." Love, trust, and obedience work together.

Obedience is a sacrifice

God almost always requires something of us that goes against our old man of sin nature, the flesh. Obedience to the Spirit of God nails our flesh to the cross. Galatians 5:17 reads, "For the flesh lusts against the Spirit, and the Spirit against the flesh: and these are contrary one to the other: so that you cannot do the things that you would."

Obedience wars against our sense of self-importance, our ambitions for power, position, and possessions. I say, "Me." Obedience says, "Him." I say, "I want." Obedience often says, "Surrender."

Obedience is the act of surrendering to the lordship of Jesus Christ. We have to be willing to suffer loss if we are to learn obedience to God. Even Jesus had to learn obedience the hard way. "Though He were a Son, yet He learned obedience by the things He suffered" (Heb. 5:8). Whatever keeps us from going through the cross to resurrection life is an enemy of the cross.

Jesus is our example of obedience unto death. He also provides us with the grace-power to be willing and able to make such sacrifices of self. He said, "Take my yoke upon you, and learn of Me; for I am meek and lowly in heart: and you shall find rest for your souls. For My yoke is easy and My burden is light" (Matt. 11:29-30). What seems impossible to us becomes possible when we step out in faith and obedience.

We obey the word

Obedience to God has to do with living by the word of God. It has to do with taking God at His word—believing that God said what He meant and meant what He said.

There are many principles in the word of God that we are to obey just because He said so. Here are some clear-cut starting points of obedience in God's word.

Specifically, when it comes to family, the wives are to submit themselves to their own husbands, as unto the

Lord. Husbands are to love their wives, even as Christ also loved His assembly of called-out-ones, and gave Himself for her (Eph. 5:22-25). Husbands are to dwell with their wives according to knowledge and understanding, giving honor to them (1 Pet. 3:7). Children are to obey their parents in the Lord; to honor their fathers and mothers; and the fathers are not to provoke their children to wrath: but bring them up in the nurture and admonition of the Lord (Eph. 6:1-4).

The dad seeks to obey the word of God in all things.

We obey the Spirit

Romans 8:14 tells us that the sons of God are those who are led by the Spirit of God. The word of God gives us general principles for guidance. But sometimes we need a more specific word from God. For this word, we pray. We listen for that still small voice within our spirits. We wait for witnesses and agreement in the word and from others. We test the motives of our hearts. We search our consciences.

Then, we act on faith. "If any of you lacks wisdom, let him ask of God, who gives to all men liberally, and do not doubt, and it shall be given to him" (Jas. 1:5). We get up in the morning, surrender our lives over to His will, ask Him to take charge of our day, and trust Him to do so. We have a piercing desire to obey God in every aspect of our lives.

We trust that "the steps of a good man are ordered by the Lord: and He delights in his way" (Ps. 37:23). We rest in the confidence that God will not allow us to make a mistake even if we make a mistake, because "we know that all things work together for good to those who love God, to those who are the called according to His purpose" (Rom. 8:28).

God is an exacting God

We now presume to know something of God, His word, His will, and what obedience to Him will require of us. It is time to obey. In the act of obedience, we find that He is an exacting God.

Jesus told a parable about three individuals who were each given a different amount of money by a nobleman. The one with the least returned to the nobleman without an increase, and said, "I feared you, because you are an exacting man: you take up what you did not lay down, and reap what you did not sow" (Luke 19:21). The nobleman in this parable portrays a God who requires what is due Him.

God wants us to obey Him explicitly. Obedience is doing what He says, doing it when He says to do it, doing it how He says to do it, and doing it for as long as He says to do it. It is for our well-being that we do so.

Obedience is righteousness

Abraham believed God and God deposited righteousness in his spiritual bank account. Righteousness is being in right standing with God. We are in right standing with God when we are standing in faith. Abraham was made righteous because he believed in what God was doing and acted on what God said.

James 2:17 says, "Even so faith, if it has not works, is dead, being alone. Yes, a man may say, 'You have faith, and I have works: show me your faith without your works, and I will show you my faith by my works.'"

Obedience is the action (or works) of faith. Without obedience faith is dead. Obedience is righteousness in motion. We find out what God wants, then we love and trust Him enough to step out in faith to do the very thing He asks.

Obedience releases the power

Obedience to God releases the power of God. He empowers and blesses His plans, not ours. His works are accomplished by His strength. Our works will have to be accomplished by our own strength. His works endure for all eternity. Our works perish with us. His works are lively. Our works are dead.

Paul writes, "Every man's work shall be made manifest: for the day shall declare it, because it shall be revealed by fire; and the fire shall try every man's work of what sort it is. If any man's work abide which he has built thereupon, he shall receive a reward. If any man's work shall be burned, he shall suffer loss: but he himself shall be saved; yet so as by fire" (1 Cor. 3:13-15).

Any works that are not built upon the foundation of Jesus Christ will be burned up as wood, hay, and stubble (vv. 11-12).

Obedience releases the blessings

The blessings of God are also associated with obedience to God. Deuteronomy 28:1-14 lists all of the blessings that were to come upon the Israelites and overtake them if they hearkened to the voice of the Lord their God:

They were to be blessed in the city, the field, the fruit of their body, the fruit of their ground, the fruit of their herds. They were to enjoy the increase of their cattle, the flocks of their sheep, their basket and their store. They were to be blessed when they went in and when they went out. The Lord would cause their enemies who rose up against them to be smitten before their face: they would come out against them one way, and flee before them seven ways. The Lord was to command the blessing upon them in their storehouses, and in all that they set their hands to do. He was to bless them in the land which the Lord their God was giving them. The Lord was to establish them as a holy people unto Himself, as He had sworn unto them. All the people of the earth would see they were called by the name of the Lord and would be afraid of them. The Lord was to make them plenteous and was to open unto them His good treasure—the heaven to give the rain unto their land in His season and to bless all the work of their hand. They would lend to many nations and not borrow. The Lord was to make them the head, and not the tail; and they were to be above only and not be beneath if they hearkened unto the commandments of the Lord their God, which He commanded them to observe and to do.

The fifty-four verses following these blessings list the things that would come upon them under the curse of disobedience. A reversal of the blessing takes place.

Obedience to God keeps the family together and releases the Father's blessing upon the family. Disobedience results in the disintegration of the family, ushering in the curse.

Israel rebelled against God and was, consequently, severed from Him. The curse of disobedience consumed the blessing of obedience. When the family breaks down and we lose sight of God's eternal purposes, we lose His power and fall prey to the curse.

The dad is a man of obedience. He stands in the gap for his family in order for his family to be the recipients of God's love, mercy, grace, power, and blessing.

PROCESSING GUIDE

Who has been an outstanding model of obedience in your family life?

How did that person's obedience impact your family life?

What is something God has asked you to do that you have been obedient to do regarding your family life?

How did that or any other act of obedience to God cost you something of self?

What is something God has asked you to do that you have been disobedient to do regarding your family life?

How has that or any other act of disobedience to God cost you something?

Write your thoughts and feelings about the ideas presented in this chapter.

Chapter 13

THE POWER OF AFFIRMATION

Beads of sweat tracked through the dust on Bill's face as he mowed the grass under the sweltering Kansas summer sun.

"Mom," he remembers, "was off doing something with the women, and dad was in the house. It was lunch time.

"'Son, come on in,' Dad bellowed from the kitchen door. His commanding voice matched his frame. 'Your mom left some beans and cornbread for us. Let's eat.'

"I raced to the wash basin, scrubbed my hands, splashed water on my sunburned face, and headed for the kitchen. I couldn't believe dad had actually set out plates and silverware for the two of us. He already had a glass of cold milk poured and sitting next to my plate.

"'Sit down, let's eat together.' His callused hand pointed to my ladder back chair. I sat. He prayed. We ate.

"We bantered back and forth with each other. Then something began to happen. We met each other that day as man to man. It was a time of real communion.

"He wiped a crumb of cornbread from the corner of his mouth, folded his napkin, and laid it carefully on the table. Then he looked me straight in the eye and asked, 'Would you be willing to go out to the wells with me today to work?' He was a production foreman at Shell Oil Company.

"'Yes, sir.' I answered.

"I will never forget it. I was 15 years old. Up to then, he had disciplined me and treated me like a child. But something changed that day. We had one of the deepest communions that I've ever had with anyone. And it started over a bowl of beans and cornbread. Something very powerful happened in the spirit between my dad and me. I had been received as a son coming of age.

"I had an intimacy with him that we hadn't shared before. We were able to discuss things that had depth to them, even spiritual things. I even had the freedom to disagree with him. Sometimes we'd get in heated discussions and Mom would get upset. We'd look at her, turn to each other, and laugh because we knew where we were with each other. I wasn't afraid of him anymore.

"The Lord moved in his heart that day. He saw that it was time. We had communion and I was affirmed."

An affirmation is a firm and positive declaration that someone or something is valid and true. We all need to be affirmed. We need someone in respected authority over us to validate us so we can say, "Hey! I'm for real. Take me seriously." Our parents, and especially the dads, are the most powerful force in our lives to impart that affirmation or withhold it from us. If dad has not done it, it is hard for us to receive it from anyone else.

I spent most of my life trying to please other people, trying to gain their approval, hoping that someone, somewhere would validate me. I did not believe that I could please even my own mother because I had not been affirmed by my dad. He never spoke disparaging words against me so far as I can remember. But a child needs affirmation, and failure to get it feels like disapproval.

Affirmation gives us the sense of who we are because we know whose we are. When we know whose we are, we develop confident personalities and are better able to receive the blessing that comes with family. The lack of affirmation in our lives causes us to emerge into insecure, doubtful, fearful, and at times enraged personalities. We find it more difficult to receive the blessing, in part because the power of blessing is not even present. We are under the curse. Curses are the opposite of blessings. Affirmations as well as the absence of them are a power that can have a profound effect upon us throughout our lives.

Sure and lasting affirmation, validation, blessing, and confidence are found within the context of the family and the power of *the dad.*

The affirmation of Jesus

We look to Father-God for our model to see how He affirmed His only begotten Son, Jesus Christ.

The power of affirmation was spoken over Jesus long before He was born. Isaiah 9:6 prophesied, "For unto us a child is born, unto us a son is given: and the government shall be upon His shoulder: and His name shall be called Wonderful, Counselor, The Mighty God, The Everlasting Father, The Prince of Peace."

God spoke the blessing of affirmation over Jesus again through the angel Gabriel when he visited the virgin Mary. The angel came to her and said, "You shall conceive in your womb, and bring forth a son, and shall call His name Jesus. He shall be great, and shall be called the Son of the Highest: and the Lord God shall give to Him the throne of His father David: and He shall reign over the house of Jacob forever; and of His kingdom there shall be no end" (Luke 1:26-33).

The blessing of affirmation over Jesus was spoken again through Elizabeth, the mother of John the Baptist and the cousin of Mary, when Mary went to visit her. "And she spoke out with a loud voice, and said, 'Blessed are you among women, and blessed is the fruit of your womb'" (Luke 1:42).

Jesus was born and the power of God's blessing of affirmation continued to soak Him. Joseph and Mary took baby Jesus to the temple in Jerusalem to present Him to the Lord as their first-born male according to the law. Also in Jerusalem was Simeon, a just and devout man, who took Jesus up in his arms, and blessed God, and said, "Lord, now let Your servant depart in peace, according to

Your word: for my eyes have seen Your salvation which You have prepared before the face of all people; a light to lighten the Gentiles, and the glory of Your people Israel." Joseph and his mother marveled at those things which were spoken of Him. (See Luke 2:25-33.)

Approximately thirty years later, Jesus went out to John in the wilderness to be baptized by Him. John, speaking by the Spirit, had already been confirming the ministry of Jesus by saying, "I indeed baptize you with water unto repentance: but He who comes after me is mightier than I, whose shoes I am not worthy to bear: He shall baptize you with the Holy Ghost, and with fire" (Matt. 3:11).

When John baptized Jesus, the scriptures say that Jesus came up out of the water and saw the heavens opened and the Spirit of God descending upon Him like a dove. Father-God spoke from heaven declaring, "You are my beloved Son, in whom I am well pleased" (Mark 1:11).

It is affirming enough to hear dad say, "You are my son." It is even better to hear him say, "You are my beloved son." But to hear dad say, "You are My beloved Son, in whom I am well pleased," is quite complete.

At this moment in time, Jesus was affirmed, approved, confirmed, validated, verified, and anointed for ministry by His Father in heaven.

From that time on nothing could shake Jesus. He knew who He was because He knew whose He was. He knew what His mission was. His Father's affirmation declared His destiny. For He, as the Son of God, was also the Lamb of God. His Father had blessed Him with the power of affirmation.

Owning the affirmation

After His affirmation at the Jordan and the temptation in the wilderness, the gospel of Luke tells us that Jesus went to the synagogue as was His custom on the Sabbath. He was handed the book of Isaiah. He scrolled to what is now our chapter 61, verses 1-2. The passage is cited in Luke 4:18-19: "The Spirit of the Lord is upon Me, because He has anointed Me to preach the gospel to the poor; He has sent Me to heal the brokenhearted, to preach deliverance to the captives, and recovering of sight to the blind, to set at liberty those who are bruised, and to preach the acceptable year of the Lord."

Jesus, knowing who He was as the beloved and acceptable Son of God, closed the book, gave it back to the minister, and sat down. A hush fell across the assembly. Their eyes were fixed on Him in anticipation of His next words. Jesus broke the silence with an awesome declaration about Himself. "This day," He said, "is this scripture fulfilled in your ears." (See Luke 4:20-21.) Jesus declared who He was and, in the process, owned the power of affirmation on His life and ministry.

The confidence of affirmation

When Jesus made this declaration, silence prevailed for a moment as they pondered the implications of what He had just said. Then, I imagine, the mumbling began, one by one. "What did He say?" "What did He mean?" They became more audible. "Is this not Joseph's son?"

Their amazement turned into wrath when He further prophesied that they would reject Him. He said to them, "No prophet is accepted in his own country." Hearing this, they mobbed Him, pushed Him out of the city, led him to the brow of the hill upon which their city had been built, and were going to throw Him off. But they couldn't do it. Luke tells us that He passed through their midst and went His way. (See Luke 4:22-30.) Can you envision the confidence and assurance He had within Himself to walk away like that? The power of God's spoken word of affirmation was upon Him and He knew it.

Our need for affirmation

Most of us live our whole lives waiting to hear daddy say through one voice or another, "You are my son, I love you, and am very pleased with you." Perhaps most of our fears, weaknesses, waverings, confusions, identity crises, and inner pain would vanish at the sound of those words from daddy's lips. Most of our dysfunction in this life is the result of this affirmation deficit in our lives.

The story of the movie *Mr. Holland's Opus*[22] illustrates my point very well. Holland, a teacher, loved his music and lived for it. All he ever wanted for himself was to have the freedom to write the music he heard inside himself.

Because Holland's teen-age son, Cole, was born deaf, his hopes of sharing his love for music with his son had been shattered. Consequently, he did not give much time to Cole but gave himself to his students.

Holland returned home one day, grieving the death of John Lennon, and got into an argument with Cole. He started to explain to Cole that Lennon had been killed, but passed it off. "You wouldn't understand."

Cole persisted in trying to get his attention.

"He wants to tell you something, and he wants to be sure you understand," Mom explained.

"Couldn't we do this another time?" Holland sulked.

"No!" insisted Cole.

Mom interpreted Cole's sign language: "Why do you assume that John Lennon's death would mean nothing to me? Do you think I'm stupid? I know who John Lennon is."

"...I never said that you were stupid."

"You must think so if you think I don't know who the Beatles are or any music at all. You think I don't care about what it is that you do or what you love? You're my father. I know what music is. You could help me to know it better, but no. You care more about teaching other people than you do about me."

Visibly shaken by Cole's confession, Holland realized

---

[22] *Mr. Holland's Opus*, written by Patrick Sheane Duncan, produced by Ted Field, Michael Nolin, and Robert W. Cort, directed by Steven Herek; An Interscope Communications Polygram Film Entertainment Production in association with the Charlie Mopic Company, presented by Hollywood Pictures; A Steven Herek film (1996).

what his lack of validation had done to his son. Their moment of reconciliation came later when Holland sang John Lennon's song at Cole's school and dedicated it to Cole. "Close your eyes. Have no fear. The monster's gone, he's on the run, and your daddy's here."

The joy of mutual acceptance brought tears to the eyes of both father and son as Holland sang the last line: "Beautiful, beautiful, beautiful, beautiful Cole."[23] Cole had the affirmation he always needed from his dad.

An ounce of approval from the lips of dad can carry a child a long way. No matter what happens to him, no matter what others may think of him, he is okay because his daddy said so.

Hebrews 1:5 says regarding Jesus, "For unto which of the angels did He say at any time, 'You are My Son, this day have I begotten you?' And again, 'I will be to Him a Father, and He shall be to Me a Son?'"

Jesus knew who He was and what He was all about because He knew whose He was. He was not the least persuaded, even by the devil himself, to be caught up into pride, power, riches, position, lust, self-pity, confusion, or other such self-indulgences.

I question whether Jesus could have withstood His sufferings had He not been bathed in His Daddy's affirmation.

Soul hunger

If we did not get that affirmation from our dads, we will seek it elsewhere. We will try to get it through academic achievement, career advancement, show business, financial success, power positioning, religious performance, relationships, psychological counseling, going along with the crowd—any way possible. But these will never deliver.

There was a time when I knew very well that the

---

[23]*Beautiful Boy*, written by John Lennon.

anointing of the Holy Spirit was upon me as I preached, yet I still wanted the approval of my wife. I liked it when other people complimented me but I wanted to hear it from her. "Honey," I imagined her saying, "you were really good today. That was the most anointed message ever. Nobody can preach like you."

Driving home after the service I would impatiently wait, "bustin'" to ask, "Well, what did you think? How was the message today?" That translates into, "Was I good or was I good?!" I knew better than to do that. I knew I shouldn't have needed her approval. I knew it was not her place to affirm me. So I held it in.

She would shuffle a little in her seat and I knew she was ready to spread it on thick. I figured she was just taking her time to find those choice words by which she would pay me the highest possible compliment. "You know, dear, I was a little uncomfortable when you said ...." Pop went the ego!

Had I received approval from my dad when I was a kid, I wouldn't need her approval now. It wouldn't even occur to me to ask for it. It wouldn't matter what she or anyone thought. I would have known who I was because I would have known whose I was. I would have been the son of my father who was well pleased with me.

Truth is, my wife constantly affirms me and that's good, because I need constant affirmation. My little bucket has holes in it.

We cannot affirm ourselves. Self-affirmation is artificial and worthless. It doesn't work. Ironically, when *the dad* affirms the "me" in us, the "me" no longer has to be the center of our self-focused universe. We no longer have to affirm ourselves or try to manipulate others into affirming us.

The God affirmation

If we were not affirmed in childhood, we will seek the approval of others and thereby are likely to enter into

119

unworkable relationships. We may be addictively drawn into disapproving, abusive relationships. We will want to evaluate those relationships and make some hard choices:

We can choose not to expect others to affirm us.

We can choose to protect ourselves from abusive relationships that continue to make us feel worthless.

We can choose to relate to others and be under authorities who are more naturally nurturing and affirming.

We can work on our own choices to affirm others.

But most of all, we can choose to turn to our Father in heaven who is the only real source and power to affirm us now. Father-God stands ready to affirm us as sons. He is already saying to those of us who will receive it, "You are My beloved son in whom I am well pleased."

We may never feel release or fulfillment in anything we do until we hear and receive the power of God's affirmation upon us.

Affirming our own

Having been affirmed, or even appreciating the need for it, convicts us to make sure that we affirm the members of our own households.

Sons and daughters both need the power of dad's affirmation. Many experts believe that homosexuality is primarily the result of a lack of relationship with the same-sex parent. This lack of bonding with the same-sex parent leaves a vacuum that the adult child seeks to fill in a same-sex partner. Nevertheless, the man, and especially the dad, is the one who affirms the masculinity of the sons and the femininity of his daughters.

We dads will want to seek the counsel and wisdom of our heavenly Daddy to know how to affirm, validate, approve, confirm, verify, and bless our own children individually. We cannot cookie-cut affirmations. Affirmations are powerful only when they speak the truth. Different children have different attributes which we will want to notice and bless.

God-words

There is power in the spoken word, especially if that word is a God-word. God-words are what we say because we are persuaded that is what God would say or is saying. God-words edify, encourage, strengthen, empower, build faith, and are expected to be accomplished. We can depend upon God to fulfill what He says. It is His job to fulfill what He says, not our job. Our job is to agree with His word in faith and say what He says in confidence.

How can we know what a God-word is? We can read the Bible. It is full of promises that we can claim over our children.

We can also pray in faith, wait, and listen for God to inspire us with a word. A word from God agrees with the scriptures, edifies, encourages, and sets us free. James 1:5-6a asserts that, "If any of you lack wisdom, let him ask of God who gives to all men liberally...and it shall be given him. But let him ask in faith, not wavering."

Parents, and especially dads, have enormous power over their kids. What we say or do not say can determine what they become. It is a matter of life or death to them.

We bless them with our affirmations and curse them with our disapprovals. Even the silence of saying nothing whispers the curse of disapproval.

More power

Numerous affirming things can be done to give others more power to live secure and successful lives.

We can speak positive, edifying, and constructive words in truth and sincerity.

We can appropriately hug and touch family members.

We can show trust.

We can recognize them for who they really are.

We can accept, love, and appreciate them regardless of their differences, uniqueness, and individualities.

We can foster a sense of belonging where they know that "you are freely mine and I am freely yours." That is to say, "This is my family. I belong here. I am at home here. I know who I am because I know whose I am."

We can authenticate them by saying and doing things that cause them to know that they are for real.

We can acknowledge, and accept their real feelings.

We can care for them, love them, and attend to them.

We can show forgiveness and mercy when needed.

We can listen to them with caring ears.

We can applaud their successes.

Affirming action

Affirmation sometimes involves more than speaking flowery words. We need to back our words with action. I can say to my son, "You are a good carpenter" then hand him a hammer. I can say to my daughter, "You have great musical talent," then provide her with music lessons. We affirm the unique attributes we discover in them as individuals.

A continual process

Affirmation is not a one-time blessing we speak over our own. It is how we genuinely feel about others all of the time even when we are angry at them or disappointed in something they did.

I brought home six bottles of beer in a paper bag when I was a teenager and hid them in my closet. I knew my mother must have seen them. I asked her years later why she never said anything to me about it. I shall never forget her answer: "I knew that wasn't you." She was right.

The dad is an affirming personality. He is positive, upbeat, always finding the good even in a bad situation. He instills confidence. He does not criticize, accuse, blame, or shame. When his children become adults, they know who they are and whose they are because daddy has declared it.

PROCESSING GUIDE

Write about any statement or action by your dad that contributed to your affirmation.

How has that given you confidence?

Write about any statement or action by your dad that made you feel disapproved.

How has that affected your confidence?

Whom have you been expecting to affirm you that you must now decide will never do so?

From what abusive relationships do you need to protect yourself?

How will you protect yourself from those abusive relationships?

Who is a nurturing and affirming authority to whom you can relate?

Whom are you responsible to affirm in your relationships?

Are you willing and ready to wait upon God as Father to affirm you? Talk to Him about that. Ask Him to affirm you.

Write your thoughts and feelings about the ideas presented in this chapter.

Chapter 14

A MAN OF BLESSINGS

"**O**n our way back from Haiti, the Holy Spirit spoke to my heart to take my son, Kel, aside and bless him," Bill said.

"The Lord had shown me the importance and power of family, and how blessings and curses are passed down through the fathers more so than the mothers.

"Kel and his wife, Lorraine, came by soon after we arrived home. I directed him toward the staircase and whispered, "Could we go down in the family room? There's something the Lord wants to do."

"'Sure, Dad,' Kel agreed.

"We sat down facing each other. I laid my hands on his head and began to speak what I heard the Father saying to him.

"'I am pleased with you and want to impart this blessing through your dad here on earth. I have called you to this place of business where you now work. You are a leader of men and I want you to be blessed with wealth, not riches, but wealth. You will soon find favor with those who are in authority over you in your work. Listen to them, but your first priority is to listen to Me. This business is blessed because the man who owns it has a heart of love for those who are in his employment.'

"Within months, Kel was asked by the owner of the company to be its president.

"'Of course,' Kel answered with reserved enthusiasm. 'But I'm sure the other men will question my age and the short time I have been with the company.'

"'Let's present it to them,'" replied the owner.

"The other men suggested they wait at least five years. Kel was willing to do that, but God had other plans. He became president soon afterwards. God has blessed him in that place. He was faithful in His promise.

"Seeing how the Lord blessed my son through me, I shyly entreated Him to speak a blessing through me on behalf of my daughter and son-in-law. But He told me to wait.

"My daughter, Melissa, and her husband, David, had been waiting twelve years to have a child. She had desired to be a mother since she was old enough to hold a doll. The doctors expressed little hope of her ever getting pregnant.

"The time came when the Lord spoke otherwise: 'I want you to ask David's father if he would join you in imparting a blessing on them, on her womb, that they might have a child.'

"'Of course,' David's father agreed.

"That Thanksgiving, we shared a meal together, then prayed that Melissa's womb would be receptive and that they would be blessed with a child who would come forth as a joy to them. Three months later, she was pregnant.

"That next Thanksgiving, we gathered to thank God for baby Kendra. And what a joy she is!" Grandpa Bill acclaimed.

James 3:8 says that "With the tongue we bless God, even the Father; and with it we curse men, who are made after the similitude of God. Out of the same mouth proceeds blessing and cursing." Then he exhorts, "My brethren, these things ought not to be." Proverbs 18:21 adds strength to this, saying, "Death and life are in the power of the tongue."

The dad is a man of blessings. He is blessed and he is the conveyor of God's blessings as they are passed on from one generation to another. He blesses and does not curse.

There is power in the spoken word. The Bible affirms,

"The wicked is snared by the transgression of his lips" (Prov. 12:13). "A man shall be satisfied with good by the fruit of his mouth" (Prov. 12:14). "...The tongue of the wise is health. The lip of truth shall be established forever: but a lying tongue is but for a moment" (Prov. 12:18-19). "He who keeps [guards] his mouth keeps [preserves] his life: but he who opens wide his lips shall have destruction" (Prov. 13:3)."Idle chatter leads only to poverty" (Prov.14:23 NKJV).

The dad blesses God

The dad is a blessed man because he is called of God to be the dad of the household. He is a blessed man because the Father's blessings flow through him.

The dad recognizes his blessings and gives thanks to God for them. He praises God for his wife, his children, his job, his house and home—no matter how humble—and gives thanks at the table for his daily bread. He is a litany of praise for all that he sees God doing or promising to do in his family. He is a positive man with a positive outlook on life. He does not take his blessing for granted.

The dad blesses himself

Though we are men of blessing, we come from shame-based backgrounds because we were born under the curse of fallen, man-of-flesh Adam. We are, therefore, bent on self-destruction and death which is compounded by the sins of the fathers. Add to that any possible rejection we may have suffered at conception or birth, the possible curses spoken over us growing up, the condemnation of our own sins, the demons in our lives, and the hurtful people in the world. Feeling disrespect for ourselves and perpetuating the bad feelings we have about ourselves is common. Whatever we feel on the inside will eventually be spoken out of our mouths. "I'm stupid." "I'm no good." "I'm always broke." We curse ourselves with these attitudes.

Jesus said, "It is not that which goes into the mouth

that defiles a man; but that which comes out of the mouth, this defiles a man" (Matt. 15:11). What ordinarily comes out of our mouths? Negative statements? Criticisms? Judgmentalisms? Cursing and swearing? Backbiting? Prejudices, bigotries, and racial slurs? These often creep back in to haunt us. We will be judged by the way we judge others and by the standards we require of others (Matt. 7:2). As the world puts it, "What goes around, comes around."

As men of God we will want to renounce, rebuke, and repudiate these defiling words we speak out of our mouths whether we are cursing ourselves or others.

We may not see immediate results from our repentance, but things will change eventually. We will begin to plant good seed for ourselves and for the generations that follow. We want to speak blessings over ourselves and teach our family members to do the same for themselves. We want to speak blessings into all areas of our lives— spirit, soul, mind, emotions, body, health, finances, and relationships.

We want to find out from God's word what He has to say about us and say that. For example: "We are the children of God: and if children, then heirs; heirs of God, and joint-heirs with Christ" (Rom. 8:16-17). When we say what God says about us, we are in agreement with Him. The Bible says that where "two of you shall agree on earth as touching anything that they shall ask, it shall be done for them of My Father who is in heaven" (Matt. 18:19).

The dad blesses his wife

1 Peter 3:7 instructs us as husbands to dwell with our wives "according to knowledge, giving honor unto the wife, as unto the weaker vessel, and as being heirs together of the grace of life" so that our prayers might not be hindered.

I believe that I am married to the most beautiful lady in the world. I often tell her how attractive she is, even in her old paint clothes—because she is. She is gifted and I see her as God's gift to me. I recognize her gifts and receive them as complements to my lack.

I have too high a regard and respect for my wife to ever call her derogatory names such as "hag," "bitch," "ugly," or "witch." This is my wife, my gift from God. Why would I ever say anything like that against my gift from God?

Men who refer to their wives as "my ol' lady" may do so teasingly but are, nevertheless, devaluating her in her own eyes and in the eyes of others. To refer to her as "my lovely bride" is just as easy, and it speaks blessing and edification.

The dad blesses his children

Fathers have the authority and power to speak the blessing or the curse over their children. Regardless what others may call us, we believe we are who our daddies say we are. He imparts the name. That name creates an image within us. That image becomes the reality of who we are. That reality points us toward our destiny whether for good or bad. What he calls us becomes our calling.

Margaret had been raised to believe that she could never live up to her father's expectations. So, Can't-Do-Anything-Right became the name that scripted her life. She medicated her insecurities and pain with frivolous shopping.

This childhood scripting led her into the arms of a man much like her father who hurled his own brand of shaming insults at her, "Can't-Do-Anything-Right, this house is a mess!" "Where did you get those awful shoes?" "Can't you control those kids?" "What's wrong with you?"

Then, one day in prayer, a moment of divine insight lit her countenance as her heavenly Father spoke to her heart saying, "Because I have redeemed you, your new name is You-Can-Do-No-Wrong." "Good morning, You-Can-Do-No-Wrong!" "Have a joyful day in the Lord, You-Can-Do-No-Wrong."

Rather than fulfilling a script that had led her down the dismal path of despair, Margaret can now look forward to allowing Christ within her to be fully revealed through her. Her life is no longer about who others say she is but who Father says she is. Moreover, her life is all about Him. He is her destiny.

We recall that God changed Abram's name to Abraham. It means "father of a multitude." If we spoke Hebrew, that is what we would be saying every time we mentioned his name. We would be reciting the covenant blessing God had spoken over him.

My children are divine gifts bestowed upon me just as is my wife. Therefore, I want to bless them by calling forth their virtues and good qualities.

We dads want to discipline our children in strength, confidence, and consistency, but we never want to control them by calling them "stupid," "bad," and "clumsy," or using such remarks as "you always" and "you never." These make indelible impressions upon their minds and emotions that can mark them for life. A child is blessed and edified when we praise them for their good points. "You are so smart." "You are a good boy." "You are a happy little girl."

We often become what is spoken over us and what we speak over ourselves, and others become what we speak over them—whether blessings or curses. We encourage others with edifying words—even calling forth those things that do not exist as though they do.

The dad turns the mistakes of his children into opportunities to teach them. He assures them of their place in the family, of their talents and gifts, attractiveness, uniqueness, and tells them daily what a joy and blessing they are to him.

The dad pronounces blessings over his children by revelation knowledge and the faith that results from that. God will speak to the heart of a man who turns to Him for a word. Once we have heard from God about anything, we can expect God to give us the faith we need to stand fast in that word.

This gift of faith is different from presumptuous faith or the positive confessions of mind control. My wife says there are just a few things she knows without a doubt that God has told her. One of these has to do with her daughters. Whenever circumstances in their lives unsettle her, she turns to the promise God gave her from Isaiah 44:3-4: "...I will pour My Spirit upon your seed, and My blessing upon your offspring: and they shall spring up as among the grass, as willows by the water courses."

Two lines from a golden oldie song are quite appropriate today: "Accentuate the positive...Latch on to the affirmative."

The dad blesses others

Our blessings extend beyond the members of our own family as we bless our neighbors, friends, and extended family members.

My neighbor Alfred was a magnet for teasing. When I was around him, it came quite naturally for me to poke fun about his age or his manicured yard. His hesitant smile tried to tell me that I was tearing him down and not building him up. Persuaded by conviction, I chose to guard my tongue. He needed, as do we all, to be encouraged, strengthened, affirmed, and built up in the faith. I determined to speak only blessings to him.

Something of worth, dignity, and virtue can be found in us all. What a blessing it is to have that affirmed rather than our faults.

The dad says what God says

What a difference our lives and the lives of all others would be if we "let our utterances be as the oracles of God" (1 Pet. 4:11).

When *the dad* says what God says, he has become the conduit for the Father's blessing. We want our testimonies about ourselves and others as sons of God to line up with the scriptures. We want to say what God says about us. The word of God illuminates and edifies. We no longer want to agree with what hateful people, demons, our sins, or shame have to say. Rather, we want to own what our Father says about us. "There is, therefore, now no condemnation to those who are in Christ Jesus, who walk not after the flesh, but after the Spirit" (Rom. 8:1).

The dad finds time to study God's word to find out how Father-God talks so he can learn to talk like Him. He spends time in fellowship with the Holy Spirit to find out what specific blessings God wants to speak into his life and in the lives of his family members. Then, he will speak those.

Even in the absence of "hearing" from God this way, we can still list the virtues and characteristics we want our children to develop and speak those over them. This does not include our yearnings for them to become great football players or movie stars, but saying such things as "you are wise," "kind," or "patient." We can cultivate the fruit of the Spirit (Gal. 5:22-23) in them by exemplifying it in our own lives and calling it forth in them. We can cultivate the positive aspects we see in them as they emerge into the unique individuals that they are. Children learn what we teach them.

The dad breaks the curses

Many families are cursed generation after generation with such things as poverty, alcoholism, divorce, sexual sins, mental diseases, abandonment, ignorance, and medical problems.

We begin to break those curses by personally repenting from the sins associated with them. We renounce, rebuke, and repudiate them and any demonic influences associated with them. We stay in covenant with God. We honor our wives and our children.

How different that is from arguing, gossiping, backbiting, accusing, slandering, condemning—all of which pronounce curses. When we speak these things, we give demonic powers the authority to try to carry them out. We invite this negative, destructive atmosphere into our own homes and against the members of our own households.

When we become aware of these practices, we can begin to do the opposite. We practice telling the truth instead of lying. We practice saying "I can" instead of "I can't." We practice blessing those things and people we want to curse.

When we see defects of character in others, we want to bless what God says about those people instead of what their defects say about them. Perhaps it is God who has given us insight to see the weaknesses of others. If so, why would He do that? So, we can criticize and condemn our brothers? That is arrogance and pride saying, "I'm better than they." Or is it so we might be thrust into a pool of mercy and intercession? Not a bad idea!

The dad breaks curses through repentance and blessing others with the word of God's love.

Reconnecting family lines

I thought my son had said that our participation in a gathering for men had healed our relationship. So, I asked him what had happened to cause that. He quickly corrected me and said that the relationship had already been healed. But he now understood that the curse of "non-existent male model" had been broken.

"Was it like the curse of abandonment?" I suggested.

"No," he insisted, "it's more like what I said—the curse of a non-existent male role model and curse of divorce over the family name."

He explained that it was as though the Newbold name was now established for the generations to come, that his dad had taken his place as the patriarch of the family and had a son and grandsons to carry on the name.

"Somewhere back," he surmised, "a curse was put on the family name, probably as the result of the sins of the fathers. That set off a cycle of degeneration that stole a positive male model from the family. But now God has given that back. There is a new beginning for this family name."

It gave him a renewed sense of stability and identity. He now had roots and branches to his family tree. "This is something that only God can do," he added. "Greatness has always come down through families. A patriarch builds something great and his sons either carry it on or corrupt it." I was quite taken by his insight.

He concluded, "The dad in a family cannot be a patriarch to those who do not recognize and receive him as such. The same thing is true with God. He is the Patriarch of all. God, as Father, will always love his kids, but He will never impose Himself upon them. He allows them the liberty to either recognize Him as Father-God, or reject Him. If they recognize and receive Him, they will be blessed of Him. But if they choose not to recognize and receive Him, they will be choosing the curses for themselves."

Until now, we had known little about my dad and his side of the family. Ironically, bits of knowledge about his life began coming to me unexpectedly, inspiring me to piece as much of them together as I could. I realized my search was more than a passing interest in genealogy. This was God reestablishing the Newbold name for those of us who have suffered the disconnection of abandonment. As my son had said from his point of view: "There is a grandfather Newbold, a father Newbold, I am a father Newbold, and I now have sons." God has reestablished our lineage.

The gospels of Matthew and Luke carefully document the genealogy of Jesus—linking Him to the throne of David. We are all firstborn sons of God through Jesus Christ—that is the only lineage that matters spiritually. Yet, family is important. Being connected is important. Marriage and family were the first institution of God. The blessings and curses are passed down through families.

Without the blessing, a family will die under the curse. Nations die when family life is corrupted.

The Father's blessing

We all need the Father's blessing. We need that significant moment in time when dad lays his hand upon our heads and pronounces the blessing upon us, saying what he hears Father-God saying over us. When that happens, we are validated and affirmed, and have our identities solidified. We belong.

"Daddy was dying," Frances wrote. She said he had been an alcoholic all of his life. He had a serious fall requiring surgery, and her mother told her it could be the end. "That is when I started to pray for God to give me Daddy," she said. She visited him everyday as he went back and forth between the hospital and the nursing home for the seven months before he died. "God gave me every request I had made of Him concerning my father. He gave me Daddy for the remainder of his life. He allowed me to share the Word with him so he could understand it. He allowed me to be with him when he accepted Christ. He gave me the blessing I had always wanted from my father."

About the blessing, she said, "When he came back from the hospital I asked Daddy if he remembered in the Bible where a blessing was given to the children. I told him the story and then asked him if he would give me a blessing. He said, 'Yes, I will.' So, I went to the head of his bed and laid my head down for him to place his hand there, and he said, 'Lord, thank you for this loving daughter and will You bless and keep her.' I cannot tell you how it made me feel inside to have had my father do this. I only know that I now feel complete as his daughter. It is the most cherished memory that I have of my father with me. This was one of the very last things he did before he died."

God is sovereignly returning *the dad* to the children so he can pronounce the blessing upon them. In all those cases, however, where dad has died or is permanently unavailable to us, we can and must go to the Source Himself for the Father's blessing.

Imparting the blessing to the sons is, as much as anything, an impartation of *the dad* power—the Father nature of God within the man. The dad who imparts *the dad* power will always be with his sons even when he departs from them because this deposit of God as Father remains in them. When the sons need the counsel of their father, they will find it within themselves.

PROCESSING GUIDE

What blessings were spoken over you as a child?

How have those impacted your life?

What curses were spoken over you as a child?

How have those impacted your life?

How have you spoken the blessing over your family members?

How have those blessings impacted their lives?

What curses have you spoken over your family members?

How have those curses impacted their lives?

List the blessings you would like God as Father to impart to you. Ask Him to extend His hand at His will and do so.

Then, when you believe it is the appropriate time, ask the Lord to give you His words as you lay hands on your own children and pronounce the Father's blessing upon them.

Write your thoughts and feelings about the ideas presented in this chapter.

Chapter 15

A Man of Peace: A Man of War

Keeping civil peace is far different from having the peace of Christ. Civil peace may be possible through the use of force, but as soon as those who enforce the peace are removed, civil disobedience returns.

Peace by force cannot change lives. Only the inner peace of the indwelling Christ can change lives and attitudes. Military and police occupation are no longer needed once lives are changed by the indwelling presence of the Prince of Peace. Military and police occupation have to be put in places where Christ is absent.

Even where Christ is present, we have an adversary to peace. Satan and his emissaries of deceit can still play havoc with our physical, emotional, social, financial, relational, and spiritual peace. He has to be confronted, oftentimes daily, in order for the man of peace to keep his peace. The godly man of peace must necessarily be a man of war.

It sounds like a contradiction of terms to say that the godly man of peace has to be a man of war. Jesus, according to Isaiah 9:6, is the Prince of Peace. He is also pictured as a mighty warrior. He appeared to Joshua before the destruction of Jericho with His sword drawn and announced that He was the commander of the army of the Lord (Josh. 5:13-15). Jesus is portrayed as a warrior by the apostle John in Revelation 19:11-16: "And I saw heaven opened, and behold a white horse; and He who sat upon him was called Faithful and True, and in righteousness He judges and makes war. His eyes were as a flame of fire, and on His head were many crowns; and He had a name written that no man knew, but He Himself. And He was clothed with a vesture dipped in blood: and His name is called The Word of God. And the armies which were in heaven followed Him upon white horses, clothed in fine linen, white and clean. And out of His mouth goes a sharp sword, that with it He should smite the nations: and He shall rule them with a rod of iron: and He treads the winepress of the fierceness and wrath of Almighty God. And He has on His vesture and on His thigh a name written, 'KING OF KINGS, AND LORD OF LORDS.'"

Just as Jesus is a man of peace and a man of war, so is it with *the dad.*

Man of peace

The dad is first a man of peace. He has that peace of God that passes all understanding (Phil. 4:7). This peace of Christ is the only peace that endures.

The dad is also a peacemaker. Jesus said, "Blessed are the peacemakers: for they shall be called the children of God" (Matt. 5:9).

The man of peace must be at peace with God, himself, and others. He ministers the peace of Christ to others to the extent that the Prince of Peace resides within him, and to the extent that he is at peace with himself.

The man of peace keeps his peace because peace is part of who he is as *the dad.* He keeps his peace by not allowing another to take it from him. He keeps his peace and is able to keep the peace of his family.

Man of war

The Strategic Air Command of the U. S. Air Force has as its motto, "Peace is our profession." It seems incongruous that men of war who fly machines of destruction should call themselves peacemakers. However, it is their ability to destroy the enemies of peace that insures peace.

This concept holds true in the Kingdom of God as well.

In order to be a man of peace, *the dad* must, ironically, be a man of war. He must be prepared to confront his adversaries. Jesus said, "When a strong man armed keeps his palace, his goods are in peace: but when one stronger than he shall come upon him, and overcome him, he takes from him all his armor wherein he trusted, and divides his spoils" (Luke 11:21-22).

Jesus, our example, confronted and defeated His adversaries. According to 1 John 3:8, "...the Son of God was manifested that He might destroy the works of the devil." Paul's letter to the Colossians says about Jesus, "Having spoiled principalities and powers, He made a show of them openly, triumphing over them in it" (Col. 2:15).

When the children of Israel came into the promised land under the warrior leadership of Joshua, they were required to take the land from the occupants a little at a time. They were to destroy the nations and their idols. (See Deut. 7.) The land was to be secured for God as God's inheritance for them.

Israel had victories and defeats. Their victories were associated with their dependence upon God. Their defeats came as the result of their unbelief, their sin, and their attempts to take matters into their own hands.

The land had not yet been secured in the days of King David. He completed the job. He was called a man of blood because of his many battles. But because of King David's warfare, his son King Solomon and all of Israel enjoyed peace on all sides of her border (1 Kings 4:24). Many battles had to be fought and won by David and his mighty men of valor before this peace was secured.

What Joshua and David had to do in the natural realm, we have to do in the spiritual realm. "For though we walk in the flesh, we do not war after the flesh: for the weapons of our warfare are not carnal, but mighty through God to the pulling down of strongholds" (2 Cor. 10:3-4).

There really is an enemy in the spirit realm who intends to destroy the family of God. One of his main targets is the destruction of the family unit itself. We must accept this reality and equip ourselves to do effective spiritual warfare.

Two realms and two kingdoms

Two very real kingdoms exist in the spirit realm that cannot be seen by the eye of natural man: the Kingdom of God and the kingdom of darkness.

Colossians 1:13 tells us that God "has delivered us from the power of darkness, and has translated us into the kingdom of his dear Son." The apostle Paul's mission to the Gentiles was "to open their eyes, and to turn them from darkness to light, and from the power of Satan unto God..." (Acts 26:18).

1 Peter 2:9 confirms that we were once in darkness but are now in God's light: "But you are a chosen generation, a royal priesthood, a holy nation, a peculiar people; that you should show forth the praises of Him who has called you out of darkness into His marvelous light."

Jesus is the King of the Kingdom of God, and Satan is the head of his kingdom. "And if Satan cast out Satan, he is divided against himself; how then shall his kingdom stand?" (Matt. 12:26).

Ephesians 2:2 reads, "...Wherein in time past you walked according to the course of this world, according to the prince of the power of the air, the spirit that now works in the children of disobedience."

Satan, the prince of the power of the air

There really is a spirit entity called Satan (Job 1, 1 Chr. 21:1, Matt. 4:10) and the devil (Matt. 4:8, Rev. 12:9). He is not equal to God nor Christ. He was created by God, rebelled against God, and was cast out of heaven to serve the purposes of God. He can do nothing that God has not allowed him to do. He is under the authority of God because all things are under the authority of God.

139

In Revelation 12:9, we find that the devil, Satan, is the great dragon that was cast down, who "deceived the whole world." Satan's main tactic is to get us to believe that he does not exist. He can get away with his evil in our lives and in the world when we foolishly believe that he is not real.

We need to settle this issue that Satan really does exist. We need to be well educated, trained, and equipped in spiritual warfare. We do not ever need to fear the devil if we are of God "because greater is He who is in us, than he who is in the world" (1 John 4:4).

Surely Satan knows that the eternal plan of God is to bring many sons to glory, sons who are of the nature and character of His pattern Son, Jesus Christ. Surely he knows that God intends to have a family of sons for Himself. His main objective is to thwart the will of God by trying to destroy the Son of God and the sons of God.

His attack has been and always will be on the destruction of family, fathering, and sonship. Everything else he is accused of doing in the world is simply designed to thwart that eternal purpose of God in one manner or another. Here are some scriptural examples.

Moses is often seen as a type of Jesus in his role as the deliverer sent to remove Israel from bondage in Egypt. Pharaoh is seen as a type of Satan in that he wanted to keep them in bondage. Egypt is seen as a type of the world and sin. When Pharaoh saw that the sons of Israel were great in number and mighty, he ordered all of the newborn sons of the Israelites to be killed (Ex. 1:7,16,22).

Next, we find Herod the king, in the time of Christ, who, when he was told that the King of the Jews had been born in Bethlehem, "sent forth, and slew" all the male children in that area from two years old and under (Matt. 2:16). What was foreshadowed in Moses became a reality in Jesus.

Finally, Revelation 12:1-6 tells us about the woman giving birth to the male child. The dragon waits to devour this child as it is born, but her child is caught up to God. The woman in this passage represents the general assembly of called-out-ones. The male child represents those many sons God will bring to glory. The dragon is Satan. (I believe Satan is already trying to destroy the "male child" through voluntary abortions—1.5 million babies every year in the United States alone.)

In all three of the scriptural cases cited above, Satan kills many babies but fails to destroy God's anointed. Yet, he was and is determined to attempt it.

We have experienced a vicious attack against the family in the past few decades. Satan will attempt to destroy the family through sin, sickness, disease, poverty, war, crime, occult practices, alcohol, drug abuse, lust, divorce—whatever results in the decapitation of the family, the removal of the head—the husband and dad.

All the more reason for the shepherd of the family to be a man of war to ward off the destroyer of God's people.

Hierarchy

Satan has a hierarchy of spirits that do his bidding for him. They are under his authority to carry out his deceiving schemes. Ephesians 6:12 identifies them as principalities, powers, rulers of the darkness of this world, and spiritual wickedness in high places.

Powers and principalities can rule as strongholds over nations, cities, religions, and institutions. These powers and principalities can also rule over churches, denominations, and religious sects.

They are puppet masters that manipulate all manner of evil in the world; such as poverty, violent crime, addictions, illicit sex, out-of-wedlock births, and suicide. They influence us to war against each other. For this reason alone, many marriages end up in divorce; families are split apart; people lie, cheat, and steal from each other; people manipulate, use, abuse, and murder one another; nations and ethnic groups war against each other.

Demons

Satan cannot be at all places at all times. Most of us are too insignificant for Satan to even know who we are, believers or not. Demons, on the other hand, are Satan's emissaries that involve themselves in the lives of individuals.

There seem to be hordes of demon spirits. The gospels tell of one man who had so many demons they were called Legion, which was a Roman military division with 3,000 to 6,000 soldiers (Mark 5:9; Luke 8:30). Jesus cast out seven demons from Mary Magdalene (Mark 16:9; Luke 8:2).

Demons operate under the principles of the kingdom of darkness whether they are consciously aware of it or not. They may not be very smart. They just do according to what they are. The Bible refers to them as unclean spirits, as evil spirits, and as seducing spirits.[24]

The Bible makes it clear that human beings can be possessed (Matt. 8:16) or oppressed (Acts 10:38) by demons.

These evil and unclean spirits can cause problems in all areas of our lives. They can tempt us to sin and cause us to be sick, diseased, infirm, and mentally and emotionally disturbed. They can cause hindrances in our finances and relationships.

Believer's authority

Jesus has given believers authority over demon spirits. Without a doubt in my mind, *the dad* has this authority, especially when it comes to his household.

Jesus can give this authority because He has all authority in heaven and earth. Philippians 2:9-11 declares, "Wherefore God also has highly exalted Him, and given Him a name which is above every name: that at the name of Jesus every knee should bow, of things in heaven, and things in earth, and things under the earth; and that every

---

[24]Unclean spirits: see Matt. 10:1; Mark 1:27; 3:11; 5:13; Luke 4:36; 6:18; Acts 5:16; 8:7; Rev. 16:13-14. Evil spirits: see Luke 7:21; 8:2; Acts 19:12-13. Seducing spirits: see 1 Tim. 4:1.

tongue should confess that Jesus Christ is Lord, to the glory of God the Father."

He has given believers the authority "to tread on serpents and scorpions, and over all the power of the enemy" with the promise that nothing shall by any means hurt us (Luke 10:19). He has given us the keys of the kingdom of heaven: "Whatsoever you shall bind on earth shall be bound in heaven: and whatsoever you shall loose on earth shall be loosed in heaven" (Matt. 16:19).

Believers can cast demons out of other people; non-believers do not have that authority. (Read Acts 19:13-16.) Exorcism is not a technique or a ritual. It does not have anything to do with being pious or religious. It is a matter of simply having the authority in Jesus' name and believing it. We have that authority by being in Christ Jesus as born-again believers. Without this authority, we are powerless.

We can bind up demons, but we cannot bind up Satan. Satan is not under our authority. He is under God's authority. Jesus has given us limited authority.

Demons are associated with sin. They have a legal right to oppress or possess us through the sins we commit or through the sins indirectly committed against us. Parental rejection before birth or any physical, sexual, and emotional abuse against children after birth are examples of indirect sin.

Casting out demons is a sign and a wonder. Mark 16:17: "And these *signs* shall follow those who believe; in My name they shall cast out demons..." We find this demonstrated by the apostle Paul when he cast out a spirit of divination in the name of Jesus Christ from a young girl who had followed him around and grieved him for many days (Acts 16:16-18).

Nevertheless, Jesus told His disciples not to rejoice in the fact that the spirits were subject to them, but rather rejoice because their names were written in heaven (Luke 10:20). We want to avoid fascination with Satan, evil spir-

its, or any part of darkness and avoid giving more credit to
the devil than is due him.

Demons are, nonetheless, a very real and present danger to us and our family's well-being. We need to know how
to cleanse ourselves, our houses, and our family members
from the defilement of demon spirits.

The nature of our warfare

Spiritual warfare involves different tactics and
weapons. Some situations call for the repentance of sin
and confession of it to others in accountability. Some situations require deliverance. Others require prayer and intercession. Some situations require that we stand in faith,
or that we praise and worship, or that we bind and loose,
or that we pray for the deep healing power of God. At all
times, we are to submit to God, resist the devil, and walk in
holiness.

Holiness toward the Lord is the ultimate weapon in our
arsenal against our spiritual enemies. It turns defeat into
victory. Holiness is another word for sanctification. Both
words mean separation. We are to be separated unto the
Lord from sin, the world, the flesh, and Satan.

Holiness is not something we can accomplish in our
own strength—trying to live by a code of "do's" and
"don'ts." Holiness is the process whereby the Holy Spirit
works to conform us into the image of Jesus. Our part is to
cooperate with Him through repentance and obedience; to
follow our Lord who said, "If any man will come after Me,
let him deny himself, take up his cross daily, and follow
Me" (Matt. 16:24).

Once we are committed to the laid-down life of obedience to Jesus, we will turn away from our sins and those
temptations that keep us in bondage to the evil one. We
cannot serve two masters. Either Jesus is master, or sin.
Jesus sets us free; sin enslaves us.

Unless we repent and walk in holiness, all else we try
to do to battle against Satan and his hosts will be futile.

Demons will find our house swept clean but empty. They will enlist seven more worse than themselves and return to occupy our lives. (See Matt. 12:43-45.) We fill our lives with the word and Holy Spirit of God and obedience to Him.

Fighting this unseen enemy requires that we dress ourselves with the armor that God has supplied: "Put on the whole armor of God, that you may be able to stand against the wiles of the devil...that you may be able to withstand in the evil day, and having done all, to stand. Stand therefore, having your loins girded about with truth, and having on the breastplate of righteousness; and your feet shod with the preparation of the gospel of peace; above all, taking the shield of faith, wherewith you shall be able to quench all the fiery darts of the wicked. And take the helmet of salvation, and the sword of the Spirit, which is the word of God" (Eph. 6:11, 13-17).

The more we walk in truth, righteousness, the gospel of peace, faith, salvation, and the word of God, the more prepared we will be to do battle against Satan and his cohorts.

"Follow peace with all men, and holiness, without which no man shall see the Lord" (Heb. 12:14).

Warfare of the mind

The mind is Satan's battlefield. For this reason we engage in effective spiritual warfare by "casting down imaginations, and every high thing that exalts itself against the knowledge of God, and bringing into captivity every thought to the obedience of Christ" (2 Cor. 10:5).

Every sin begins as a temptation in the mind. James 1:14-15 explains, "But every man is tempted, when he is drawn away by his own lust, and enticed. Then when lust has conceived, it brings forth sin: and sin, when it is finished, brings forth death."

If we love the Lord with all of our minds, we will give ourselves over to the Lord. Otherwise, we will continue to give ourselves over to the enemy of our minds.

This enemy does not always go away. We may have to battle certain disturbances to our peace for the rest of our lives. But victory is possible. We can now do something about these temptations that invade our minds. We have the weapons of choice, prayer, binding and loosing, accountability, resistance, faith, etc. The enemy would like to condemn us for merely having the temptation, but the word of God keeps us in perfect peace. Satan is defeated.

We can choose what we think about. Paul wrote, "Finally, brethren, whatsoever things are true, whatsoever things are honest, whatsoever things are just, whatsoever things are pure, whatsoever things are lovely, whatsoever things are of good report; if there is any virtue, and if there is any praise, *think on these things* [italics mine]" (Phil. 4:8).

Jesus is the Prince of peace. When we receive Him, we receive His peace. If we have the mind of Christ as the Bible says, we should have peace of mind. If we are to maintain that peace of mind, we have to be willing to wage war against whatever disturbs that peace. For the man of peace is a man of war.

PROCESSING GUIDE

Make three columns on a piece of paper:

In the first column, list those things in your life and your family's life that disturb the peace. Examples: lustful thoughts, rage, a defiant/rebellious child, relational conflict, accusations, backbiting, cursing, manipulation. Review James 3:13-18.

In the middle column write what you think is the cause or source of those disturbances that correspond with those things you wrote in the first column. Examples: exposing yourself to pornography, false expectation of others or self, peer influences, excessive use of mood altering chemicals, etc.

146

In the third column, write what you think might be the appropriate weapon of warfare against those disturbances that correspond with those things in the first column. The examples that are given in this chapter are: repentance of sins, confession of sins to others, submission to the ministry of deliverance, prayer and intercession, standing in faith, praise and worship, binding and loosing, submission to the deep healing power of the Holy Spirit, or resisting the devil.

Apply the appropriate weapons during the coming days and weeks and note the effects. Be prepared to try different weapons at times.

Write your thoughts and feelings about the ideas presented in this chapter.

Chapter 16

A MAN IN ACCOUNTABILITY

The guys meet every Tuesday night in Steven's basement. They have been doing it for years now. Drinking coffee. Laughing. Crying. Praying. Sometimes they go past midnight to make sure everyone has his chance to share. God has been known to do mighty miracles on behalf of these men who cared enough about their lives and their loved ones to hold one another accountable week after week.

These guys are not alone. Many men are gathering in accountability groups seeking integrity. They study together, draw upon each other's collective wisdom and experiences, pray together, grow together, and mentor one another in love. Collectively, they make up for the absence of *the dad* model.

Accountability is living in relationship with others as an open book whereby others can read our lives, and, moreover, influence the writing of them to produce character and integrity.

Willingness to be accountable

Accountability has to begin with a willingness for certain others in our lives to know all about us. They need to know our darkest secrets—those sins that so easily beset us—not in order to shame and condemn us or spread gossip about us but to help us maintain a lifestyle of repentance, to encourage and strengthen us.

Whatever is hidden in darkness stays hidden as long as it is kept secret. Sin thrives in the darkness of secretiveness and denial. But once that sin is exposed to the light, it is eradicated by the light. It cannot survive in the light of repentance and confession.

Accountability in relationships with others will be phony and fruitless if we are not willing to be transparent. We will only continue to deceive ourselves and try to deceive others into believing we are OK when, in fact, we are not.

Honesty with self

Before we can allow others to snoop around in our lives, we will want to do a little snooping on our own. We will want to own the truth about those sins that we have been pretending do not exist. We will stop justifying them. Knowing the truth about ourselves is difficult for many of us, because we were not taught how to know what we feel, think, want, or believe. How, then, can we expect to tell others?

We begin by taking a long, serious, honest look at ourselves and owning up to some threads of truth. We admit that we do have problems: sins, addictions, obsessive-compulsive behaviors, and bad attitudes. And maybe, just maybe, we are the cause of those problems.

We own those realities about ourselves. We own the fact that our lives are unmanageable, that we are powerless apart from God, that we are willing to change or be changed by God, and that we need accountability in our lives. Such confessions lead to repentance. Repentance has to do with changing our minds and the direction of our lives.

The more we learn about our defects of character, the less these defects are likely to rule our lives. We can solve only those problems that we know exist.

But not everything about us is bad. We have good traits as well. The more we know about our gifts, talents, and attributes, the more we can release those to God for Him to use in His Kingdom. He wants it all.

As we come to know who we are, we will be more prepared to submit ourselves to God and to others for accountability.

Hitting the "bottom"

It is not until we "hit bottom" that any of us are likely to repent. Repentance begins when we come to the end of ourselves. The depth we must go to hit "bottom" is different for each of us. It may depend on our stubbornness.

Norman sat in our kitchen as we offered to pray with him about his problems. We wanted so much to help him turn his life around. He was homeless, hungry, broke, and jobless. His only possessions were the clothes on his body. He would walk for hours at night, sometimes in the rain, and sleep standing up as he leaned against a wall.

"Norman, are you content with your life?" I asked.

"Yes," was his simple reply.

"That's it?" I asked. I was smitten with disbelief. "If that's so, there isn't anything I can do for you."

The depth we must go to "hit bottom" may depend upon how deeply rooted the sin is; for the deeper the sin, the harder it will be to uproot it. When that sin is generational, as many of them are, that tap root runs even deeper.

Though we do not always like what those sins do to us, they feel like buddies to us. We do not want to give them up. We may not be finished with them, and we will give to God only those things we are finished with. We are rarely finished with anything until it begins to give us more pain than pleasure. So, God may allow certain things to happen as the result of that sin to bring us to the end of it, to bring us to the end of ourselves.

Submitting to a circle of mentors

Different mentors serve different purposes in our lives. We may discover that we already have a circle of mentors. Some guide us spiritually and morally. Some provide professional services, such as doctors, lawyers, and accountants. Others are available for emotional and psychological counseling. Different mentors are qualified to be there for us in different ways. We want to be sure to receive from these mentors according to their purposes. We would abuse our dentists by telling them about our financial problems. That is not their expertise nor is it any of their business—unless, of course, we owe them money.

Our wives, if we are married, are mentors in certain areas of our lives. My wife knows everything she needs to know about me for the sanctity of our marriage. She knows me physically, spiritually, socially, sexually, ethically, financially, and morally. She knows me like a book. I am automatically accountable to her for every doughnut I am not supposed to eat, every cup of coffee I am not supposed to drink, every grain of salt I'm not supposed to use, and every caretaking finger I am not supposed to lift.

My wife is a positive influence in my life because she is the one who lives with me day in and day out. She is loving, caring, and accepting of me. She is not critical and judgmental. She knows how to "stand by her man." She does not preach, nag, or try to rescue me. She is almost too willing for me to make my own decisions, knowing full well that I am willing to bear the consequences of my mistakes. Yet, in the midst of the consequences, she is a rock. Besides, she often tells of how she goes over my head in prayer to commit things to my Head, Jesus, when she thinks I'm doing wrong; and she is able to leave it there.

Yet, there are times when I need other men, not my wife, with whom I can talk things over.

Submitting to trusted brothers

Finding the right guys for this kind of accountability is not an easy task. It takes time to find other men who have proven themselves to be trustworthy and are willing to connect in openness and honesty. We want to be cautious about airing our dirty laundry to just anyone. Many people cannot be trusted with our honesty. They, themselves, are still in sin and denial. As long as they can redirect attention from themselves by slandering others, they will do it.

I gave my testimony to a group of churchmen once. I think they were looking me over as a prospect for assistant pastor. I wanted to be honest and open with them. I told them of my involvement in some occult activities for a short time during my atheistic period and how that bondage led me to back to the Lord. They could not handle that information. How could a man once ordained to ministry fall away that far? Could he be trusted again? Was he crazy? I am not sure what they thought; but, whatever it was, the door was closed to prospective ministry after that.

While we need to exercise caution, we need not be ruled by what other people think about us. It is none of our business what others think of us unless, of course, we have harmed them and need to make amends. If we ever fear what others might think about us, we will likely find it impossible to open up to other trusted brothers.

Submitting to accepting brothers

Until we become accepting of one another without judging and criticizing, we are not likely to reveal our deepest needs. I doubt that I could have made an accountability circle out of those churchmen to whom I gave my testimony.

We want to show as much grace, love, and acceptance to one another as our Lord has shown to us. Yet, accepting one another does not mean that we condone our sins, not at all. The goal of accountability is to help one another live above sin. For "God did not send His Son into the world to condemn the world but that the world through Him might be saved" (John 3:17).

It is vitally important that we men get together for accountability in honesty, openness, and acceptance. Finding other men with whom we are willing to be mutually honest, open, and accepting is like finding buried treasure. It is worth buying the whole field to have it.

Submitting to committed brothers

Men who are willing to get connected with one another in honesty, openness, and acceptance will want to commit themselves faithfully to one another, themselves, God, and the process.

This involves a commitment of time. Men in accountability have to commit to a time to be together and commit to being faithful to one another in this time. Brothers in accountable relationships can be called at two o'clock in the morning. They will climb out of bed, pick us up at the phone booth by the corner liquor store, and drink a cup of coffee until daybreak if that is what it takes.

God has blessed me over the years with a few men who are as close to me as brothers. We are hundreds of miles from each other; yet, we will drive across several state lines to "be there" for each other. We know about each other's weaknesses and strengths. We love and support each other. We share our joys and our sufferings. We do not judge and condemn each other, but neither do we let each other get away with junk in our lives.

I believe that God has appointed men with whom He will connect us. He wants this for all of us. He does not want men ruling over men, but men who are submitted one to another as peers. Such men may already be in our lives. Let us pray and ask God to open our eyes to see them. Let us take measured steps to get to know one another at a more intimate level. Let us build a relationship of trust and be willing to commit to one another in sincerity.

For the purpose of accountability, it is not necessary to seek out other men who have the same sin as we do. It is OK if they do, because we will understand one another's vulnerability. But it is equally powerful to have others in our lives who can be strong in areas where we are weak, and we can be strong in areas where others are weak. Romans 15:1 instructs us: "We then who are strong ought to bear the infirmities of the weak, and not to please ourselves."

We can gain strength from one another when we are connected with men who know our weaknesses and vulnerabilities, who can call us at any time they feel impressed to do so and ask, "How are you doing in that area?" If we are doing well, we say so. If we are not doing well, we say so and let that brother minister to us.

Faithfulness and loyalty are disciplines that have to be perfected with practice. Let us begin practicing faithfulness and loyalty with our brothers in accountability. Let us be faithful in the little things—being faithful to be at our meetings with them, being on time, staying the time, and praying faithfully. Learning faithfulness in the group will have its ripple effect upon our faithfulness at home.

Submitting to praying brothers

We can always find others who are willing to listen to us, to load us down with advice, or to pour us another drink. It is more difficult to find others who will get down on their knees and pray with us. We can submit to our bartenders, barbers, doctors, and lawyers, but what we really need are prayer partners.

The more people we are able to include in our circle of mentors, the more prayer support we will have mustered for ourselves. God answers prayer, especially the fervent and effectual prayers of righteous men (Jas. 5:16). Let us pray with one another, pray for one another, pray over one another, and pray when we are away from one another. Prayer will help keep us shielded from the fiery darts of the devil.

Submitting one to another

Submission one to another suggests that we are all on common ground. Individuals who think they are beyond correction do not belong in the group. They create a climate of distrust and are unsafe to be around.

When we mutually submit one to another in a confidential support group environment, we will be more transparent and trusting of each other. God will release more of His mercy and grace. He will give us wisdom and insight. A climate will be created for God to send His word of edification, healing, deliverance, transformation, and empowerment. Psalm 107:20 says, "He sent His word and healed them, and delivered them from their destructions."

Taking responsibility for ourselves

Even though we are in accountability to others, we cannot expect others to live our lives for us. We can and probably should inventory our lives to see what made us like we are. But we cannot hide behind what others have done to us as an excuse to stay in sin. It is time we grew up and took responsibility for ourselves.

My son went through a trying time many years ago which compelled him into a counselor's office. His counselor helped him to see what effects his parents and their past had upon molding him into the person he had become. Blaming us was his excuse for not working on his own issues.

I had repeatedly asked him to forgive me. Nothing changed until one day I said, "Son, I accept responsibility for what happened to you as a child. I made serious mistakes with you. But you are now a grown man and your own person. You can no longer hide behind me. You must now take responsibility for yourself." He told me several times afterwards how that admonishment changed his mind and his life.

I tend to be a caretaker in the dysfunctional sense of that term. By caretaker, I mean one who does for others what they could and should be doing for themselves. Caretakers do these things in order to find their significance in the approval of others. Though we never get that approval, we compulsively continue to caretake. We tend to other people's business when it is not our business to do so. We tend to other people's business because we do not have a clear sense of our own boundaries. We do not know what is and what is not our business.

I had been conditioned to be this way during my formative years. I could blame mother for making me that way and continue to caretake others, or I could take responsibility for myself and stop acting that way.

I need other men who know this about me—men who will call me up short when they see me messing up. But those other men in my life cannot live my life for me. I cannot live their lives for them. We have to take responsibility for ourselves. Until we are willing to do that, we are merely faking accountability which won't change anything.

We will want to take responsibility in all life areas: what we think, say, and do. We will want to take responsibility for our spiritual growth, physical and emotional health, finances, attitudes, and resentments. We will want to take responsibility if we get that girl pregnant, tell lies, or make mistakes. We will not shift the blame on others. We will say, "I'm sorry, please forgive me." We will take the steps necessary to make things right.

We are responsible to get help when we need it. How do we know when we need help? When God has not supernaturally intervened, and we cannot "white knuckle it" any longer.

As long as we are being honest with ourselves, we will more likely accept responsibility for ourselves. When we cease to be honest with ourselves, we will go back to faulting others for our behavior.

Submitting to God

Ultimately, accountability is an issue between the individual and God. We can pretend with one another and be in denial to ourselves, but we cannot fool God. Little good comes from pretending submission to others if we are not willing to submit to God for accountability. Only we know how true we are to stay responsible to ourselves, God, and others when no one else is looking.

PROCESSING GUIDE

Are you willing to admit the truth about yourself to yourself?

What things are you now willing to admit about yourself that you have been pretending did not exist or was not a problem?

Are you willing to commit this truth about yourself to others?

What hinders you from admitting and committing this truth to others?

What measures can you take to remove those hindrances?

How has committing a truth about yourself to trusted brothers helped you to maintain victory in that area?

How have you experienced defeat in an area of your life because you were unwilling to commit that truth to another?

List those whom you could trust with your secrets.

If you are not already in an accountability group, are you willing now to call a few other guys?

Make the calls.

Write your thoughts and feelings about the ideas presented in this chapter.

Chapter 17

A MAN IN SURRENDER

In the natural realm we defeat our enemies when they surrender to us. In the spirit realm we defeat our enemies when we surrender to the lordship of Jesus Christ. He goes before us to drive out our enemies. He fights our battles for us.

Surrendering to the lordship of Jesus Christ is yielding ourselves as wet clay into the hands of the Master Potter for Him to mold us into the man He wants us to be. His potter's wheel is spinning and His kiln is fired in His readiness to bring us forth. Nevertheless, He will not violate our wills. He waits until we truly want Him to be Lord of our lives.

We want God to mold us into the best husbands and dads possible. We can do some things on our own to bring about change, but most changes take shape in the palm of the Potter's hands. The pot is powerless to mold itself. We surrender our lives over to the care of God who has the power to change us. We may be able to change what we do, but only God can change what we are.

The Bible teaches us that we are spirit, soul, and body. Paul writes in 1 Thessalonians 5:23, "And the very God of peace sanctify you wholly; and I pray God your whole spirit and soul and body be preserved blameless unto the coming of our Lord Jesus Christ." *The dad* surrenders all of who he is—spirit, soul, and body—to all of who Christ is. This includes every aspect of every life area over which *the dad* is responsible.

Surrendering our spirits

We pay little attention to the fact that we are spirit, soul, and body. We live our lives feeling good or feeling bad, being well or being sick, laughing or crying, being hungry and eating, running around through the mazes of our lives, being who we are for better or worse.

We think about things. We learn things. We forget things. We feel things. We get angry, sad, happy, fearful. We feel things emotionally and we feel things bodily. But we may never think of ourselves as being anything other than a whole, integrated human being. We do not even think about that. We go about living, acting and reacting, hoping, praying, waiting, rushing here and there.

Then, one day we come face to face with the reality of Jesus Christ in the realm of the spirit man. We suddenly realize that He is the Lord of lords and Savior of the world, or, as Peter confessed, "You are the Christ, the Son of the living God" (Matt. 16:16). Jesus breaks through to us with the reality of His presence. We are called up short in the way we are living. We are told that we need to surrender our hearts and lives to Him and declare Him as the Lord of our lives. We may say the words of surrender by repeating a sinner's prayer and find that our lives are changed. Something becomes a part of us that we can never walk away from. We are born again from above by the Holy Spirit of God in our spirit-man. We surrender our spirits to Him.

Surrendering the strongholds of our souls

When we first surrender to the lordship of Jesus Christ, it is probably in the middle of some crisis in our lives. We come to the end of ourselves. We have nowhere else to turn, so we finally turn to God. God is usually the source of last resort. At that time, we feel as though we have truly turned everything over to Him.

However, most of us find later, even years later, that there are things in our lives we still need to surrender. These are strongholds over which the enemy of our flesh has had particular control, things we still want to hang on to. We may still be ruled by our thought life, fears, angers, depressions, greed, resentments, or lusts. We may be ruled by tragedies that occurred to us as children. We may be ruled by money and the lust for things. We may be ruled by an addiction, a relationship, or a sin. We have to become willing to surrender these things in our lives.

As we surrender, we give God permission to work in these areas. Pulling down these strongholds is a gradual work of the Holy Spirit as He works the lordship of Jesus Christ into our daily lives. We begin to realize that true and lasting changes are taking place within us. As we go along, He continues to reveal new areas that need to be surrendered.

So, we have been born again in our spirit man, and the Bible tells us that we are now being conformed into His image (Rom. 8:29). It is as though that seed of new life planted within the spirit of man is sprouting and growing outwardly to produce fruit in all areas of the soul.

Surrendering the body

Surrendering our spirits to God when we were born again was a sacrifice of self. Surrendering our souls (that is, our personalities: mind, emotions, and will) to be conformed into His image was a sacrifice of self. The greatest sacrifice, however, occurs when we are willing and able to lay down our bodies. "I'll live for You, God," we declare; but God asks, "Will you die for Me?"

Paul wrote in Romans 12:1, "I beseech you, therefore, brothers, by the mercies of God, that you present your bodies a living sacrifice, holy, acceptable unto God, which is your reasonable service."

Revelation 12:11 says that those who overcame the accuser of the brethren (Satan) are characterized by these three things: "They overcame him by the blood of the Lamb, and by the word of their testimony; and *they loved not their lives unto the death*" (italics mine).

We come to this death by totally surrendering to God all of who we are or ever hope to be—spirit, soul, and body—and allowing Him to be Lord over every area of our lives. We overcome the pitfalls in our lives to the extent that we surrender them to the lordship of Jesus Christ.

Surrendering to God's will

Surrendering has to do with yielding to the Lord in obedience, praying, "Not my will, Lord, but Yours." Surrendering to God's will always requires some action. It is never a matter of being passive, laying down and playing dead. The word surrender itself suggests that we are having to let go of something we want very much to hold on to.

Surrendering is a heart issue. We come to that place where Jesus is the only thing there is, where we seek His face and not His hand, where we want to do His will more than we want our own lives. We invite Him to take full control.

Getting very particular

We want to allow the Holy Spirit to get very particular with us over the things we surrender to Him. Some of the things we thought were hidden from the scrutiny of our heavenly Father will sooner or later have to be brought to the light of the cross of Christ.

We want to surrender to God our minds, thoughts, emotions, resentments, fears, worries and anxieties, expectations, and self-centeredness. We want to surrender our defects of character, sins, addictions, codependency, self-destructive behaviors, and bad habits. We want to surrender our wills, needs, aspirations, and plans. We want to surrender our bodies, health, eating, and sex lives. We want to surrender our abilities, professions, careers, jobs, and ministries. We want to surrender our relationships, family, friends, and co-workers. We want to surrender our finances, property, and possessions. We want to surrender our time, and our past, present and future lives. We want to

161

surrender even our religious attempts to save ourselves.

We surrender all to God on the conviction that He is Lord of all, that He is all in all. He is our righteousness and our salvation, our strength and joy, our justifier and our justification, our redeemer and our redemption, our sanctifier and our sanctification, our glorifier and our glorification. He is our physician, health and healing. He is our provider, our protector, the author and finisher of our faith, the apostle and high priest of our calling, the shepherd and guardian of our souls.

Purchased by God

Surrendering our all is the act of giving God what He has already purchased. Paul reminded the Corinthians, "You are bought with a price: therefore glorify God in your body, and in your spirit, which are God's" (1 Cor. 6:20). Jesus Christ paid the price for us by shedding His precious blood on the cross. It is up to us to accept or not accept that on faith.

When we declare Him to be Lord of our lives, we are saying that He now owns us entirely. We belong to Him. He has complete jurisdiction over us and all of the affairs of our lives. We live by faith in Him. He truly becomes Lord over our lives when we so yield to Him.

So, if we are ever to become the dad that God intended for us to be among other men and in the home, we must learn how to surrender ourselves over to the absolute lordship of Jesus Christ, thereby allowing Him to take all of who we are to the cross with Him. He is the only one who can perfect and mature us spiritually.

We have to surrender in all sincerity. As I said before, we will not surrender to God what we are not yet finished with ourselves.

Surrendering is a very subtle thing. We may think that we have done so, but it is something that has to take place in the spirit, not just the head. Once a thing has truly been crucified within us, we will know it.

162

Cut from the pattern Son

Jesus Christ is the Son of God. As such, He is the prototype of many sons to come. He is the pattern. Every new son has to be cut directly from Him.

We surrender all of who we are to become all of who He is. We not only become His, but we become as He is. 1 John 3:1-2 declares, "Behold, what manner of love the Father has bestowed upon us, that we should be called the sons of God...Beloved, now are we the sons of God, and it does not yet appear what we shall be: but we know that, when He shall appear, we shall be as He is."

We surrender ourselves completely over to His divine, sovereign care in order that we might be conformed into His image as sons of God (Rom. 8:29).

We die daily

The apostle Paul said of himself, "I die daily" (1 Cor. 15:31). So must we. We have to die to our own willfulness, drives, ambitions, self-centeredness, sins—everything that speaks of idolatrous independence from God.

Surrendering is a daily activity. We cannot do it once only and take for granted that these things are eternally given over to God. We always have our wills to contend with. We are quite capable of deceiving ourselves into believing we are surrendered when in fact we have taken something of ourselves back into our own hands. We want to pay daily attention to this in order to make sure we stay surrendered to the lordship of Jesus Christ in all of the areas of our lives.

The laid-down life

Surrendering this way is part of what Jesus meant when He called each of us to "deny himself, and take up his cross, and follow Me" (Matt. 16:24). It is what He meant when He said, "No man having put his hand to the plow and looking back is fit for the Kingdom of God" (Luke 9:62). It is what He meant when He said, "If any man comes

163

to Me and does not hate his father and mother and wife and children and brothers and sisters; yes, and his own life also, he cannot be my disciple" (Luke 14:26). To hate in this sense means that in all things we give preference to the will of Father-God rather than our flesh or to the expectations of others. As long as we are being ruled by what other men think of us, we will not be able to live in obedience to the Holy Spirit.

The crucified life

Surrendering to the lordship of Jesus Christ has to do with living the crucified life of Jesus Christ. Romans 6:3 says, "Don't you know, that so many of us as were baptized into Jesus Christ were baptized into his death?" This has to mean more than being immersed in or sprinkled with water. It has to do with how we live our lives. "...Our old man is crucified with Him, that the body of sin might be destroyed, that henceforth we should not serve sin" (Rom. 6:6a). We are to live crucified lives.

Living the crucified life is the only way we can come into resurrection life. Romans 6:4 says, "Therefore we are buried with Him by baptism into death: that like as Christ was raised up from the dead by the glory of the Father, even so we also should walk in newness of life. For if we have been planted together in the likeness of His death, we shall be also in the likeness of His resurrection."

We dads need to be dead to self, the world, Satan, and sin that we might be resurrected as true men of God. We need to be raised up as true husbands, fathers, heads of households, and men of integrity in the community. This is the sanctifying work of the Holy Spirit to which we surrender.

Dare to surrender

As *the dad*, we dare to live the surrendered life—dare to destroy those things which displease the Father in the fire of our passion for Him. Even if we know we might take them up again, we can exercise our wills to destroy them for now, knowing that exercise strengthens that part which is exercised (Heb. 5:14).

Let us keep the fire of sacrifice burning in our hearts and souls that we might be men who live surrendered lives, molded according to the pattern Son, by the fingers of the Master Potter.

PROCESSING GUIDE

What does it mean to you to surrender to the lordship of Jesus Christ?

Take a serious inventory of each area of your life and get honest with yourself and God. Answer for yourself:

What have I not yet taken to the cross?

Why have I not taken it?

What do I think that thing is still doing for me?

What is it going to do to me?

How might it eventually affect me? My family? My job? My spiritual life? My health? My economic future? My sanity? Other relationships?

What will it take for me to be willing to surrender it to Jesus?

Refer to the subheading in this chapter titled "Getting very particular" and determine which of these areas you are ready to surrender to the lordship of Jesus Christ.

Deliberately pray a prayer of surrender to God. Name everything to Him that you are surrendering. Repeat this daily.

Write your thoughts and feelings about the ideas presented in this chapter.

Chapter 18

A MAN WHO DOES WHAT IS RIGHT

Junior did not turn bad overnight. What started out as an occasional drunken escapade sank into a life of wantonness with the town whores. The harlot's claw gripped his mind and he had lost all reason. Leaving home was on his mind. The world had come into him and was calling him to go out into it. "Dad," he arrogantly demanded, "give me the part of the family property that belongs to me."

The father saw it coming. Perhaps he had already purposed to give Junior what he thought he wanted even before he asked. Without a word, the father divided the living between Junior and his older brother. The older brother had not asked for this. He was content in his father's house. He was content to work the fields and earn his living fair and square. But Junior! He was the unbridled one in the family.

Junior's father had prepared a better legacy for him than this. Standing by, watching while his son chose a path of excess broke his heart. Yet, he knew there was no room for correction in his son. He had to let him go. He had to give him what he asked for. It was the right thing to do under the circumstances.

Days later, Junior packed up his possessions and traveled to a foreign country where he wasted his living on wine and women. Then, depression choked the land. He lost everything. Where were his friends then? In desperation, he went to work for a pig farmer, willing to eat the husks the pigs ate. But no one would give him anything.

It took wallowing in the sty with the pigs for Junior to come to his senses. He reasoned, "Dad's hired hands have more than enough to eat, and I'm dying of hunger! I'll go to my father, and say to him, 'Dad, I did you wrong. I am not worthy to be called your son. Just let me come and work for you.'"

Ragged. Beat. Dirty. Yet, determined. He labored, one barefoot step at a time across that crusty land. He was going home.

His father longed for his son's return. Day after day, he would steal a glance toward the horizon in the hope that he might catch the silhouette of his wayward son. Finally, that day came. What joy filled his heart! He saw him coming while he was still a long way off and, in abandoned compassion, ran out to meet him. He hugged and kissed him. Such love. Such acceptance. And he did not even know, as yet, how broken and repentant Junior really was.

Junior fell at his father's feet and told him of his resolve: "I am not worthy to be called your son." Without a word, father reached down, took his hand, and raised him to his feet. He turned to one of his workers and said, "Bring me the best of my clothes for him, put a ring on his finger and shoes on his feet, and then kill that calf we've been feeding out. Let's eat and have a party."

Junior's older brother did not feel as generous toward him as did his father. He refused to join the party. When the father went to him, his son lashed out at him. "Look! I've served you all these years and never once crossed you. But did you ever throw a party for me and my friends?"

This merciful, compassionate, and generous father embraced his son and said, "You are always with me, and all that I have is yours. Don't be jealous of your brother, but be glad with me. *It was right* that we should throw a party and be glad, for your brother was dead and is alive again; he was lost and now is found." (See Luke 15:11-32.) "It was right," the father said, because *the dad* does what is right.

Knowing what is right

Knowing what is right is sometimes like groping through a fog. We desperately need God's guidance. We need His wisdom, knowledge, and understanding.

God knows our weaknesses. He is patient with us when we admit our confusion and seek His face for direction. We have a responsibility to God to find out to the best of our abilities what is good and right. Many of us do not know what is good and right because it has not been modeled for us. Yet, good models are still around, and we have our heavenly Father who is our perfect model. We can still learn.

The New Testament abounds with "one another" exhortations that define normal Christian conduct—a good place for any dad to begin. Be at peace with one another. Love one another. Be kindly affectionate with one another. Prefer one another in honor. Be like-minded with one another. Edify, receive, admonish, wait and care for one another. Bear one another's burdens. Be tender-hearted, forgiving, submitted. Teach and admonish one another. Do not speak evil against one another. Do not hold a grudge. Confess your faults and pray for one another. Show hospitality and minister your gifts to one another and have fellowship with one another.

Romans 12:9-15:7 adds to this list of things we can purpose in our hearts to do. Do not be slothful in your business. Serve the Lord. Be patient in times of trouble. Stay in prayer. Give to the needs of the saints. Bless people who persecute you and do not curse them. Do not pay back evil for evil. If your enemy is hungry, feed him; if thirsty, give him a drink. Overcome evil with good. Pay people what is due them. Do not commit adultery. Do not kill, steal, bear false witness, or covet. Walk honestly; not in rioting, drunkenness, lewd behavior, strife, and envying. Do not make any provision for lust. Bear the infirmities of the weak.

In addition to these scriptural directives, we can look to mature Christian men as good models for us. When possible, we should invite one of them into our lives for counsel. If we cannot do that, we can observe their lives from a distance and imitate what good we see in them. Each of us has something of good to model one to another.

Knowing what is right is also a matter of conscience— that something deep inside of us, that still small voice that not only tells us what is good and right but instills a desire to do what is good and right.

Doing what is right

James 4:17 informs us: "Therefore to him who knows to do good, and does it not, to him it is sin." It is one thing to know what is right and quite another to do it. We do the right thing regardless of how we feel about it, regardless of our energy level. We may not feel like mopping up the spilled milk or giving the kids a bath, but we do it anyway because it is the right thing to do. We may not want to pick up the Bible and teach our children about God, but we do it anyway because it is the right thing to do. We may not want to sacrifice our diversions and escapes to be there for the family, but we do it anyway because it is the right thing to do.

We are the ones responsible for making the right call. God wants us to be as zealous about making the right call in our family matters as we are with the referees who are making the calls for our favorite sports team. Sometimes we may need to go fishing alone. Other times we may need to take the family along. Then, there are times we need to keep the children so mom can be alone. Whatever wisdom says is the right thing to do, we do it.

When we are acting responsibly as husbands and fathers by making the right call, we create a positive atmos-

169

phere wherein we and our families can grow spiritually and personally. We become fertile ground for all of God's goodness to take root and bear good fruit.

Selfless love

Doing what is right as *the dad* is the act of laying down our self-centeredness for the well-being of others. This is *agape*-love. *Agape* is the resource of God's own life within us that is made available to meet the legitimate needs of others. It is living selflessly in relationship with others.

Jesus explained it this way: "Greater love has no man than this, that a man lay down his life for his friends" (John 15:13). He pictured it this way: "Except a corn of wheat falls into the ground and dies, it abides alone: but if it dies, it brings forth much fruit" (John 12:24). He not only was speaking of His own life and sacrificial death but of the cost of discipleship as well. Jesus defined *agape* with his own life. The death that comes as the result of *agape* is the only ground for resurrection life.

Agape says, regardless of our mood, to carry out the garbage, cut the grass, clean out the garage, change the diaper, come home after work, take the wife out on a date, pray with her, help the kids with homework, and shave on weekends. Find out what is right in your situation and do it. God rewards the price we pay for selfless love.

Agape puts us into other people's shoes. We remember how afraid we were as children when someone yelled at us or how lonely we felt when we needed a hug. We think about how mom must be feeling at the end of a child-wrenching day, how she must long for an adult conversation after confinement with the preschoolers. We reflect upon those kinds of things. We ask ourselves questions: How can I make a difference here?

The responsibility for raising the children is a partnership with dad taking the lead. Taking the lead does not mean raising our voices in anger when the kids disrupt our football game. *Agape* describes the father who, in spite of his love for the game, is willing to turn it off to play on the floor with his kids when the situation calls for it.

The dad is parented to maturity by exercise, by doing what is right in every situation. There is a saying among addicts and codependents in recovery, "We cannot think ourselves into right action; we have to act ourselves into right thinking." To the best of our ability, we do the right thing regardless of our thoughts and feelings; and, at the same time, we give room for Father-God to bring us to that place where *the dad* becomes the natural thing we do.

The time is now to catch the wind of God's Holy Spirit who is teaching men everywhere what is right. He is giving us the love, courage, power, and desire to do it. And, in the course of doing what is right for our children, we will model what our sons are to become. They will grow up with a portrait of *the dad* imprinted in their spirits.

PROCESSING GUIDE

Imagine a conversation with God as your Father. What domestic things would He counsel you to do that you are not doing? Examples: cut the grass, baby-sit the kids, clean the garage, help out in the kitchen, compliment your wife and children, eat together as a family, help the children with homework, improve your attitude, be more generous, be more saving, etc.

What things would He counsel you to stop doing that you are doing? Examples: running around with the guys, watching too much TV, being sloppy, wasting money, not paying your bills, cutting people down, etc.

What domestic things do you believe are rightfully yours to do? Are you faithful to do them?

Is your failure to help out around the house a source of conflict in your marriage?

What does your wife think you ought to be doing or not doing?

How do you justify your failure to do your part?

How would the relationship with your wife and children change if you took more responsibility around the house? If you did more for them? If you did more with them?

What decisions are you willing to make in order to do what is right regardless of your mood?

Write your thoughts and feelings about the ideas presented in this chapter.

Chapter 19

A Man Tested in Fire

W ould it not be great for God to wave a magic wand and have the stardust of fatherhood fall upon our heads, suddenly changing us from frogs to mature men of God? Yeah! Well, that is not going to happen. Father-God alone is the Source who has the power to call forth *the dad* within the man of each of us. But His ways are not our ways. He changes us by the flame of His passion and compassion for us. If we want to be changed, we must be willing to be "a man tested in fire."

Speaking through the prophet Malachi, God expresses His passion for Israel, declaring, "'Behold, I will send My messenger, and He shall prepare the way before Me: and the Lord, whom you seek, shall suddenly come to His temple, even the messenger of the covenant, whom you delight in: behold, He shall come,' says the Lord of hosts. 'But who may abide the day of His coming? And who shall stand when He appears? For He is like a refiner's fire, and like fullers' soap: And He shall sit as a refiner and purifier of silver: and He shall purify the sons of Levi, and purge them as gold and silver, that they may offer unto the Lord an offering in righteousness'" (Mal. 3:1-3).

The messenger spoken of by Malachi was Jesus. John the Baptist proclaimed Jesus as the one who would purge by fire: "And now also the ax is laid to the root of the trees: therefore every tree that does not bring forth good fruit is cut down, and cast into the fire. I indeed baptize you with water unto repentance: but He who comes after me is

173

mightier than I, whose shoes I am not worthy to bear: He shall baptize you with the Holy Spirit and with fire: whose fan is in His hand, and He will thoroughly purge His floor, and gather wheat into the garner; but He will burn up the chaff with unquenchable fire" (Matt. 3:10-12).

Jesus came to His temple two thousand years ago and He promises to come again. His second coming is spoken of throughout the Bible as "the great and dreadful day of the Lord"—great for those who are ready and dreadful for those who are not.

The Lord always comes with fire. The passage in Malachi continues: "'For, behold, the day comes, that shall burn as an oven; and all the proud, yes, and all who do wickedly shall be stubble: and the day that comes shall burn them up,' says the Lord of hosts, 'that it shall leave them neither root nor branch'" (Mal. 4:1).

Just as John the Baptist came in the spirit of Elijah to prepare the way of the Lord, so also is the spirit of Elijah coming among the body of Christ today to prepare the way for His second coming. That preparation will come in the restoration of family, just as is prophesied in Malachi 4:5-6: "Behold, I will send you Elijah the prophet before the coming of the great and dreadful day of the Lord: *And he shall turn the heart of the fathers to the children, and the heart of the children to their fathers,* lest I come and smite the earth with a curse" (italics mine).

God promises to turn the heart of the fathers to the children and the heart of the children to the fathers, and it appears from this reading in Malachi that He intends to do that in His refining fire.

Doing business God's way

Shortly after the manuscript for this book was put into the hands of several people for review, God tested me. He permitted my marriage of twenty-six years and my relationship with family members to be cast in the crucible of His refining fire.

174

An old pre-conversion offense that I had committed came to the light. It had been hidden in the hope that one day it would simply vaporize. How foolish to think we can skirt that disturbing verse that warns, "Be sure, your sin will find you out" (Num. 32:23).

Members of my family were painfully hurt. The shame, the guilt, and the speculations against me crushed me as well. "Why this? Why now, after all of these years? Surely," I thought, "this is the devil's attempt to discredit me and, thereby, this book." If the devil's matches were found at the scene of this fire, it was only because, as one Bible teacher put it, "the devil is God's ways and means committee." I should have seen it coming. God's refining fire is His way of doing business with us. Here is how He often works:

God sends His word

Psalms 107:20 reads, "He sent His word and healed them." We know about God because He revealed Himself to us. He made Himself known through such Bible giants as Abraham, Moses, King David, Elijah, Isaiah, and Ezekiel. The revelations they received fill most of the Old Testament pages. God revealed Himself in word and deed.

Jesus was God's word sent to us. In the fullness of time, God sent His only begotten Son, Jesus Christ. John wrote, "In the beginning was the Word, and the Word was with God, and the Word was God...And the Word became flesh, and dwelt among us, (and we beheld His glory, the glory as of the only begotten of the Father) full of grace and truth" (John 1:1,14).

The Holy Spirit has always been God's agent for delivering His word. Jesus, as the Word of God made flesh, consoled His disciples, saying, "When He, the Spirit of truth, has come, He will guide you into all truth: for He shall not speak of Himself; but whatsoever He shall hear, that shall He speak: and He will show you things to come" (John 16:13).

175

Paul explained to the Corinthians that God reveals things to us "by His Spirit: for the Spirit searches all things, yes, the deep things of God" (1 Cor. 2:10).

God sends His word in order to reveal Himself to us.

God changes us by His word

God sends His word and His word changes us. This change begins with the new birth experience. Belief in Jesus Christ as the Son of the living God changes us. It happened to Simon Peter when Jesus asked, "Who do men say that I am?" By revelation Peter answered, "You are the Christ, the Son of the living God." Jesus explained to him that "flesh and blood has not revealed this to you but My Father who is in heaven" (Matt. 16:16-17). This revelation changed Peter's life.

The conversion of Saul of Tarsus (also known as Paul) profoundly illustrates how God's sent Word, Jesus, can radically change us. He was on the road to Damascus breathing threats and murder against the disciples of the Lord. He had a letter in his fist to take to the synagogues there so that if he found any who were of The Way, he might bring them bound to Jerusalem.

On his way, a light suddenly shown around him from heaven. He fell to the ground and heard a voice asking, "Saul, Saul, why are you persecuting Me?" Quite shaken by this, Saul asked, "Who are you, Lord?" And He answered, "I am Jesus whom you are persecuting." Saul was struck blind and the men with him were speechless.

A few days later, his sight was restored, he was filled with the Holy Spirit, "and straightway he preached Christ in the synagogues, that He is the Son of God." (See Acts 9:1-20.) What a difference in this man!

God gives grace

God gives us grace to live according to the word He sends. Life was not a bed of roses for Paul after his conversion. He was a man on fire, and he was constantly under fire.

His tiring litany of trouble was expressed in his letter to the Corinthians as he was defending his apostolic calling. Comparing himself to the other apostles, he wrote, "Are they Hebrews? So am I. Are they Israelites? So am I. Are they the seed of Abraham? So am I. Are they ministers of Christ? (I speak as a fool) I am more; in labors more abundant, in stripes above measure, in prisons more frequent, in deaths often. Of the Jews five times I received forty stripes save one. Three times I was beaten with rods, once was I stoned, three times I suffered shipwreck, a night and a day I have been in the deep; In journeyings often, in perils of waters, in perils of robbers, in perils by my own countrymen, in perils by the heathen, in perils in the city, in perils in the wilderness, in perils in the sea, in perils among false brethren; in weariness and painfulness, in watchings often, in hunger and thirst, in fastings often, in cold and nakedness." (2 Cor. 11:22-27).

He also told of the visions and revelations he had received from the Lord, even about being caught up into Paradise where he heard inexpressible words—things that are not even "lawful for a man to talk about."

A messenger of Satan was sent to buffet him lest he should be caught up (in pride) by the things he had been shown. He called this messenger his "thorn in the flesh."

He pleaded three times that it might depart from him, but God answered, "My grace is sufficient for you: for My strength is made perfect in weakness." (See 2 Cor. 12:1-9.)

God sent His word to Paul, converted him, changed his life by the word, sent him out, and gave him grace to sustain him in the midst of his fire. God's grace saves us, keeps us, and enables us to do what He has called us to do and be. But He does that in His refining fire.

God tests His word

God uses His refining fire to test His life-changing, grace-empowering word to us.

177

God's refining fire makes us feel as though we are the ones under fire. In reality, God is testing Himself. He is testing His word and grace—not to see *if*, but to show *that*. It is not a test to see *if* we are going to make the grade, because it does not have to do with us. It has to do with God who sent His word, changed us by His word, and gave us grace to live according to His word. He wants us to know *that* His word works, *that* a change has occurred.

Isaiah 55:11 reads, "So shall My word be that goes forth out of My mouth: it shall not return unto Me void, but it shall accomplish that which I please, and it shall prosper in the thing whereto I sent it."

God is His word, He performs His word, and we are the fruit of His word. It may help us, therefore, in the midst of a trial, to remember that the fire is not about us but about God. It is about His word and His purposes being fulfilled in all eternity. To suggest that the fire is about us smacks at arrogance.

God will usually let us know what His fire is supposed to be doing so we can cooperate with Him. Stubbornness and rebellion on our part can cause us unnecessary pain.

2 Sam. 22:31 reads, "As for God, His way is perfect; the word of the Lord is tried [tested]." And Psalms 12:6 reads, "The words of the Lord are pure words: as silver tried in a furnace of earth, purified seven times." God sends His word, it does the work it was supposed to do, and then He sets His word on fire in us in order to test its integrity.

A year and a half had gone into the making of this book. Many of the revelations had come as a result of God's fire in my life. But this! This personal trial in my life was His test to show *that* He had made me into the stuff I had been writing about. Many questions needed to be answered. Would I be able to do what was right? To show love, compassion, and mercy? To be other-caring? Would I be able to put the interests of my family members before my own? Would I stand my ground against the enemy's attack? Would I be a covering for my family whether they wanted that or not? Do I now have *the dad* power? The word poured out upon these pages had to be proven in me.

The purposes of God's refining fire

Psalm 97:3 declares, "A fire goes before Him, and burns up His enemies round about." The enemies of God include such things as "adultery, fornication, uncleanness, idolatry, witchcraft, hatred, strife, wrath, heresies, envyings, murders, drunkenness" (Gal. 5:19-21).

In the midst of this fire, I was faced with a paradox: On the one hand, it felt like the enemy's attempt to discredit me and thereby the contents of this book. Furthermore, it would be a bonus entry on Satan's ledger if he could succeed in trashing my marriage.

On the other hand, this was a God-thing. What Satan would have used for evil, God meant for good. "And we know that all things work together for good to them who love God, to them who are the called according to His purpose" (Rom. 8:28). God wanted to do a deeper work in me and heal the woundedness between family members. He certainly wanted to disarm the enemy at this crucial time in my life.

This fire in my life was anything but pleasant. Each of us involved suffered our own losses. We felt everything possible but good. The pain was deep. Angers seethed. Depression veiled our perspectives. Confusion ruled our hearts and minds. Oftentimes we did not know what our thoughts and feelings were. We did not know what we ought to think or feel. All I could do at first was to pace back and forth through the corridors of my befuddled mind and cry out to God, "I don't know what to do. I don't know who I am."

Then God sent a healing word to me, saying, "You are who your Father says you are."

"That's right," I thought to myself. "I am who my Father says I am." He had already confirmed that I, too, was His beloved son in whom He was well pleased. This trial now solidified that reality in me. I stood upon the word He had given to me. He is my foundation. All other ground is sinking sand. This fire was a defining moment for me. It no longer mattered what anyone else thought of me. My Father had spoken.

"For You, O God, have proved us: You have tried us, as silver is tried" (Ps. 66:10).

Assurances in God's word

We can expect God to set His refining fire under the kettles of our lives as He begins to work *the dad* power in us. But let us take heart. In the middle of the fire, we have these assurances:

"'But now this,' says the Lord who created you, O Jacob, and He who formed you, O Israel, 'Fear not: for I have redeemed you, I have called you by your name; you are mine. When you pass through the waters, I will be with you; and through the rivers, they shall not overflow you: when you walk through the fire, you shall not be burned; neither shall the flame kindle upon you. For I am the Lord your God, the Holy One of Israel, your Savior...Every one who is called by My name...for I have created him for My glory, I have formed him; yes, I have made him....Beside Me there is no savior...There is no one who can deliver you out of My hand...Remember not the former things, neither consider the things of old. See, I will do a new thing, Now it shall spring forth; Shall you not know it? I will even make a road in the wilderness and rivers in the desert...This people whom I have formed for Myself shall show forth My praise...I, even I, am He who blotted out your transgressions for My own sake, and I will not remember your sins'" (Is. 43:1-3, 7, 11, 13, 18-19, 21, 25).

Fires come and fires die out. They never leave things as they were before. As for me, after this fire, I am settled in who I am according to My Father, determined to be what He has made me to be, focused on what He has called me to do, empowered to live a separated life, and committed to my marriage and family as never before.

For some, forgiveness comes hard. Memories never die. Nevertheless, God is strengthening our marriage and making it more Christ-like than before, and I am "confident of this very thing, that He who has begun a good work in [us] will perfect it until the day of Jesus Christ" (Phil. 1:6).

Father-God wants to make us men of valor—men who will go on with Him, who will do what He says to do, say what He says to say, and be who He has made us to be regardless of adversity.

I am convinced that Malachi 4:5-6, which prophesies that God will return the heart of the fathers to the children and the heart of the children to the fathers, is an end-time prophecy that is presently being fulfilled by the coming forth of *the dad.* Father-God is restoring family as He intended family that He might fulfill His eternal purpose to have a family for Himself.

Lay claim to this promise.

PROCESSING GUIDE

What do you think God is doing or wants to do with His refining fire in your life?

What sacrifices might you have to make in order for God to do a new work in you?

Is what God wants to do in your life worth those personal sacrifices you might have to make?

More of God usually means more fire. More fire means more power. Are you ready to pray, "More, Lord, more of You?"

Pray continually, "Father, call forth *the dad* within this man of Yours."

Write your thoughts and feelings about the ideas presented in this chapter.

CLOSURE

While studying this book, what have you learned that is different from your previous concepts about being a husband and a dad?

How has God changed things for better in your life? Your marriage? Your family?

How have you personally changed while reading this book?

Where do you hope to go from here in terms of who you are as *the dad*?

What do you now want God to complete in you?

If you are studying this book with other men, take the time now to lay hands on each other, one at a time, and ask the Father to call forth *the dad* within the man. Then, listen for the Holy Spirit to impress upon each of you a blessing that you can speak over one another.

Consider continuing on as a growth group in accountability or consider dividing into new groups in order to lead other men through this experience.